RIFLE

AND

LIGHT INFANTRY TACTICS;

FOR

THE EXERCISE AND MANŒUVRES

OF

TROOPS WHEN ACTING AS LIGHT INFANTRY
OR RIFLEMEN.

PREPARED UNDER THE DIRECTION OF THE
WAR DEPARTMENT,

BY

BREVET LIEUT.-COL. W. J. HARDEE,
U. S. ARMY.

VOL. II.

SCHOOL OF THE BATTALION.

PHILADELPHIA:
J. B. LIPPINCOTT & CO.
1861.

RIFLE AND LIGHT INFANTRY TACTICS.

TITLE FOURTH.

SCHOOL OF THE BATTALION.

Formation of the Battalion.

1. EVERY colonel will labor to habituate his battalion to form line of battle, by night as well as by day, with the greatest possible promptitude.

2. The color-company will generally be designated as the directing company. That, as soon as formed, will be placed on the direction the colonel may have determined for the line of battle. The other companies will form on it, to the right and left, on the principles of successive formations which will be herein prescribed.

3. The color-bearer may have received the color from the hands of the colonel; but if there be daylight, and time, the color will be produced with due solemnity.

Composition and march of the color-escort.

4. When the battalion turns out under arms and the color is wanted, a company, other than

that of the color, will be put in march to receive and escort it.

5. The march will be in the following order, in quick time, and without music; the field music, followed by the band; the escort in column by platoon, right in front, with arms on the right shoulder, and the color-bearer between the platoons.

6. Arrived in front of the tent or quarters of the colonel, the escort will form line, the field music and band on the right, and arms will be brought to a shoulder.

7. The moment the escort is in line, the color-bearer, preceded by the first lieutenant, and followed by a sergeant of the escort, will go to receive the color.

8. When the color-bearer shall come out, followed by the lieutenant and sergeant, he will halt before the entrance; the escort will present arms, and the field music will sound *to the color*.

9. After some twenty seconds, the captain will cause the sound to cease, arms to be shouldered, and then break by platoon into column; the color-bearer will place himself between the platoons. and the lieutenant and sergeant will resume thei posts.

10. The escort will march back to the battalion to the sound of music in quick time, and in the same order as above, the guide on the right. The march will be so conducted that when the escort arrives at one hundred and fifty paces in front of the right of the battalion, the direction of the march will be parallel to its front, and when the color arrives nearly opposite its place in line, the

column will change direction to the left, and the right guide will direct himself on the centre of the battalion.

Honors paid to the color.

11. Arrived at the distance of twenty paces from the battalion, the escort will halt, and the music cease; the colonel will place himself six paces before the centre of the battalion, the color-bearer will approach the colonel, by the front, in quick time; when at the distance of ten paces, he will halt: the colonel will cause arms to be presented, and *to the color* to be sounded, which being executed, the color-bearer will take his place in the front rank of the color-guard, and the battalion, by command, shoulder arms.

12 The escort, field music, and band, will return in quick time to their several places in line of battle, marching by the rear of the battalion.

13. The color will be escorted back to the colonel's tent or quarters in the above order.

General Rules and Division of the School of the Battalion.

14. This school has for its object the instruction of battalions singly, and thus to prepare them for manœuvres in line. The harmony so indispensable in the movements of many battalions, can only be attained by the use of the same commands, the same principles, and the same means of execution. Hence, all colonels and actual commanders of battalions will conform themselves,

without addition or curtailment, to what will herein be prescribed.

15. When a battalion instructed in this drill shall manœuvre in line, the colonel will regulate its movements, as prescribed in the third volume of the Tactics for heavy infantry.

16. The school of the battalion will be divided into five parts.

17. The first will comprehend opening and closing ranks, and the execution of the different fires.

18. The second, the different modes of passing from the order in battle, to the order in column.

19. The third, the march in column, and the other movements incident thereto.

20. The fourth, the different modes of passing from the order in column to the order in battle.

21. The fifth will comprehend the march in line of battle, in advance and in retreat; the passage of defiles in retreat; the march by the flank; the formation by file into line of battle; the change of front; the column doubled on the centre; dispositions against cavalry; the rally, and rules for manœuvring by the rear rank.

PART FIRST.

Opening and closing ranks, and the execution of the different fires.

ARTICLE FIRST.

To open and to close ranks.

22. The colonel, wishing the ranks to be opened, will command:

1. *Prepare to open ranks.*

23. At this command, the lieutenant colonel and major will place themselves on the right of the battalion, the first on the flank of the file closers, and the second four paces from the front rank of the battalion.

24. These dispositions being made, the colonel will command:

2. *To the rear, open order.* 3. MARCH.

25. At the second command, the covering sergeants, and the sergeant on the left of the battalion, will place themselves four paces in rear of the front rank, and opposite their places in line of battle, in order to mark the new alignment of the rear rank; they will be aligned by the major on the left sergeant of the battalion, who will be care-

ful to place himself exactly four paces in rear of the front rank, and to hold his piece between the eyes, erect and inverted, the better to indicate to the major the direction to be given to the covering sergeants.

26. At the command *march*, the rear rank and the file closers will step to the rear without counting steps; the men will pass a little in rear of the line traced for this rank, halt, and dress forward on the covering sergeants, who will align correctly the men of their respective companies.

27. The file closers will fall back and preserve the distance of two paces from the rear rank, glancing eyes to the right; the lieutenant colonel will, from the right, align them on the file closer of the left, who, having placed himself accurately two paces from the rear rank, will invert his piece, and hold it up erect between his eyes, the better to be seen by the lieutenant colonel.

28. The colonel, seeing the ranks aligned, will command:

4. FRONT.

At this command, the lieutenant colonel, major, and the left sergeant, will retake their places in line of battle.

29. The colonel will cause the ranks to be closed by the commands prescribed for the instructor in the school of the company, No. 28.

Article Second.

Manual of arms.

30. The ranks being closed, the colonel will cause the following times and pauses to be executed:

Present arms.	*Shoulder arms.*
Order arms.	*Shoulder arms.*
Support arms.	*Shoulder arms.*
Fix bayonet.	*Shoulder arms.*
Charge bayonet.	*Shoulder arms.*
Unfix bayonet.	*Shoulder arms.*

Article Third.

Loading at will, and the Firings.

31. The colonel will next cause to be executed loading at will, by the commands prescribed in the school of the company No. 45; the officers and sergeants in the ranks will half face to the right with the men at the eighth time of loading, and will face to the front when the men next to them come to a shoulder.

32. The colonel will cause to be executed the fire by company, the fire by wing, the fire by battalion, the fire by file, and the fire by rank, by the commands to be herein indicated.

33. The fire by company and the fire by file will

always be direct; the fire by battalion, the fire by wing, and the fire by rank, may be either direct or oblique.

34. When the fire ought to be oblique, the colonel will give, at every round, the caution *right* (or *left*) *oblique*, between the commands *ready* and *aim*.

35. The fire by company will be executed alternately by the right and left companies of each division, as if the division were alone. The right company will fire first; the captain of the left will not give his first command till he shall see one or two pieces at a ready in the right company; the captain of the latter, after the first discharge, will observe the same rule in respect to the left company; and the fire will thus be continued alternately.

36. The colonel will observe the same rule in the firing by wing.

37. The fire by file will commence in all the companies at once, and will be executed as has been prescribed in the school of the company No. 55 and following. The fire by rank will be executed by each rank alternately, as has been prescribed in the school of the company No. 58 and following.

38. The color-guard will not fire, but reserve itself for the defence of the color.

The fire by company.

39. The colonel, wishing the fire by company to be executed, will command:

1. *Fire by company.* 2. *Commence firing.*

SCHOOL OF THE BATTALION—PART I.

40. At the first command, the captains and covering sergeants will take the positions indicated in the school of the company No. 49.

41. The color and its guard will step back at the same time, so as to bring the front rank of the guard in a line with the rear rank of the battalion. *This rule is general for all the different firings.*

42. At the second command, the odd numbered companies will commence to fire; their captains will each give the commands prescribed in the school of the company No. 50, observing to precede the command *company* by that of *first, third, fifth,* or *seventh,* according to the number of each.

43. The captains of the even numbered companies will give, in their turn, the same commands, observing to precede them by the number of their respective companies.

44. In order that the odd numbered companies may not all fire at once, their captains will observe, but only for the first discharge, to give the command *fire* one after another; thus, the captain of the third company will not give the command *fire* until he has heard the fire of the first company; the captain of the fifth will observe the same rule with respect to the third, and the captain of the seventh the same rule with respect to the fifth.

45. The colonel will cause the fire to cease by the sound to *cease firing;* at this sound, the men will execute what is prescribed in the school of the company No. 63; at the sound, for officers to take their places after firing, the captains, covering sergeants, and color-guard, will promptly re-

VOL. II.—2

sume their places in line of battle: *this rule is general for all the firings.*

The fire by wing.

46. When the colonel shall wish this fire to be executed, he will command:

1. *Fire by wing.* 2. *Right wing.* 3. Ready.
4. Aim. 5. Fire. 6. Load.

47. The colonel will cause the wings to fire alternately, and he will recommence the fire by the commands, 1. *Right wing;* 2. Aim; 3. Fire; 4. Load. 1. *Left wing;* 2. Aim; 3. Fire; 4. Load; in conforming to what is prescribed No. 35.

The fire by battalion.

48. The colonel will cause this fire to be executed by the commands last prescribed, substituting for the first two, 1. *Fire by battalion;* 2. *Battalion.*

The fire by file.

49. To cause this to be executed, the colonel will command:

1. *Fire by file.* 2. *Battalion.* 3. Ready.
4. *Commence firing.*

50. At the fourth command, the fire will com-

mence on the right of each company, as prescribed in the school of the company No. 57. The colonel may, if he thinks proper, cause the fire to commence on the right of each platoon.

The fire by rank.

51. To cause this fire to be executed, the colonel will command:

1. *Fire by rank.* 2. *Battalion.* 3. READY.
4. *Rear rank.* 5. AIM. 6. FIRE.
7. LOAD.

52. This fire will be executed as has been explained in the school of the company No. 59, in following the progression prescribed for the two ranks which should fire alternately.

To fire by the rear rank.

53. When the colonel shall wish the battalion to fire to the rear, he will command:

1. *Face by the rear rank.* 2. *Battalion.*
3. *About*—FACE.

54. At the first command, the captains, covering sergeants, and file closers will execute what has been prescribed in the school of the company No. 69; the color-bearer will pass into the rear rank, and for this purpose, the corporal of his file will

step before the corporal next on his right to let the color-bearer pass, and will then take his place in the front rank; the lieutenant colonel, adjutant, major, sergeant major, and the music will place themselves before the front rank, and face to the rear, each opposite his place in the line of battle — the first two passing around the right, and the others around the left of the battalion.

55. At the third command, the battalion will face about; the captains and covering sergeants observing what is prescribed in the school of the company No. 70.

56. The battalion facing thus by the rear rank, the colonel will cause it to execute the different fires by the same commands as if it were faced by the front rank.

57. The right and left wings will retain the same designations, although faced about; the companies also will preserve their former designations, as *first, second, third,* &c.

58. The fire by file will commence on the left of each company, now become the right.

59. The fire by rank will commence by the front rank, now become the rear rank. This rank will preserve its denomination.

60. The captains, covering sergeants, and color-guard will, at the first command given by the colonel, take the places prescribed for them in the fires, with the front rank leading.

61. The colonel, after firing to the rear, wishing to face the battalion to its proper front, will command:

1. *Face by the front rank.* 2. *Battalion.*
3. *About*—FACE.

62. At these commands, the battalion will return to its proper front by the means prescribed Nos. 54 and 55.

63. The fire by file being that most used in war, the colonel will give it the preference in the preparatory exercises, in order that the battalion may be brought to execute it with the greatest possible regularity.

64. When the colonel may wish to give some relaxation to the battalion, without breaking the ranks, he will execute what has been prescribed in the school of the company Nos. 37 and 38 or Nos. 39 and 40.

65. When the colonel shall wish to cause arms to be stacked, he will bring the battalion to ordered arms, and then command:

1. *Stack*—ARMS. 2. *Break ranks.*
3. MARCH.

66. The colonel wishing the men to return to the ranks, will cause *attention* to be sounded, at which the battalion will re-form behind the stacks of arms. The sound being finished, the colonel after causing the stacks to be broken, will command:

Battalion.

67. At this command, the men will fix their attention, and remain immovable.

PART SECOND.

Different modes of passing from the order in battle to the order in column.

Article First.

To break to the right or the left into column.

68. Lines of battle will habitually break into column by company; they may also break by division or by platoon.

69. It is here supposed that the colonel wishes to break by company to the right; he will command:

1. *By company, right wheel.* 2. March (or *double quick*—March).

70. At the first command, each captain will place himself rapidly before the centre of his company, and caution it that it has to wheel to the right; each covering sergeant will replace his captain in the front rank.

71. At the command *march*, each company will break to the right, according to the principles prescribed in the school of the company No. 173; each captain will conform himself to what is prescribed for the chiefs of platoon; the left guide, as soon as he can pass, will place himself on the left of the

18 P.32

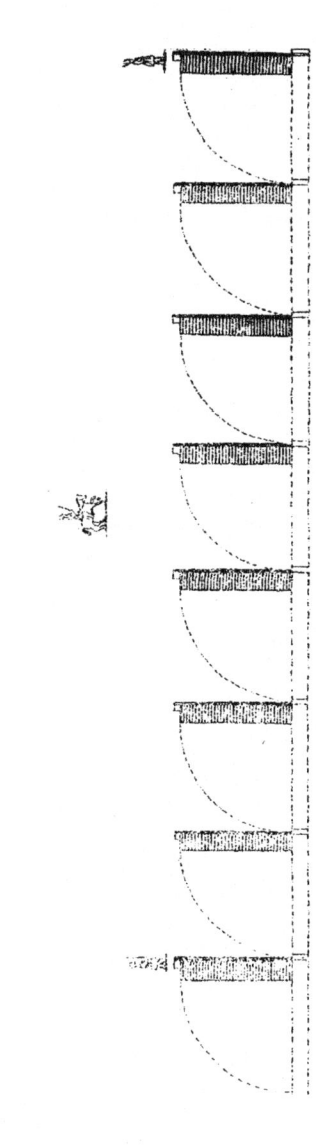

SCHOOL OF THE BATTALION—PART II. 19

front rank to conduct the marching flank, and when he shall have approached near to the perpendicular, the captain will command: 1. *Such company.* 2. HALT.

72. At the second command, which will be given at the instant the left guide shall be at the distance of three paces from the perpendicular, the company will halt; the guide will advance and place his left arm lightly against the breast of the captain, who will establish him on the alignment of the man who has faced to the right; the covering sergeant will place himself correctly on the alignment on the right of that man ; which being executed, the captain will align his company by the left, command FRONT, and place himself two paces before its centre.

73. The captains having commanded FRONT, the guides, although some of them may not be in the direction of the preceding guides, will stand fast, in order that the error of a company that has wheeled too much or too little may not be propagated; the guides not in the direction will readily come into it when the column is put in march.

74. A battalion in line of battle will break into column by company to the left, according to the same principles, and by inverse means; the covering sergeant of each company will conduct the marching flank, and the left guide will place himself on the left of the front rank at the moment the company halts.

75. When the battalion breaks by division, the indication *division* will be substituted in the commands for that of *company;* the chief of each division (the senior captain) will conform himself to

what is prescribed for the chief of company, and will place himself two paces before the centre of his division; the junior captain, if not already there, will place himself in the interval between the two companies in the front rank, and be covered by the covering sergeant of the left company in the rear rank. The right guide of the right company will be the right guide, and the left guide of the left company, the left guide of the division.

76. When the battalion shall break by platoon to the right or to the left, each first lieutenant will pass around the left of his company to place himself in front of the second platoon, and for this purpose, each covering sergeant, except the one of the right company, will step, for the moment, in rear of the right file of his company.

77. When the battalion breaks by division to the right, and there is an odd company, the captain of this company, (the left), after wheeling into column, will cause it to oblique to the left, halt it at company distance from the preceding division, place his left guide on the direction of the column, and then align his company by the left. When the line breaks by division to the left, the odd company will be in front; its captain, having wheeled it into column, will cause it to oblique to the right, halt it at division distance from the division next in the rear, place his right guide on the direction of the other guides, and align the company by the right.

78. The battalion being in column, the lieutenant colonel and major will place themselves on the directing flank, the first abreast with the lead-

ing subdivision, and the other abreast with the last, and both six paces from the flank. The adjutant will be near the lieutenant colonel, and the sergeant major near the major.

79. The colonel will have no fixed place as the *instructor* of his battalion; but in columns composed of many battalions, he will place himself habitually on the directing flank fifteen or twenty paces from the guides, and abreast with the centre of his battalion.

80. When the colonel shall wish to move the column forward without halting it, he will caution the battalion to that effect, and command:

1. *By company, right wheel.* 2. MARCH (or *double quick*—MARCH).

81. At the first command, the captains of companies will execute what is prescribed for breaking into column from a halt.

82. At the second command, they will remain in front of their companies to superintend the movement; the companies will wheel to the right on fixed pivots as indicated in the school of the company No. 185; the left guides will conform to what is prescribed above; when they shall arrive near the perpendicular, the colonel will command:

3. *Forward.* 4. MARCH. 5. *Guide left.*

83. At the third command, each covering sergeant will place himself by the right side of the

man on the right of the front rank of his company. At the fourth command, which will be given at the instant the wheel is completed, the companies will cease to wheel and march straight forward. At the fifth, the men will take the touch of elbows to the left. The leading guide will march in the direction indicated to him by the lieutenant colonel. The guides will immediately conform themselves to the principles of the march in column, school of the company, No. 200 and following.

84. If the battalion be marching in line of battle, the colonel will cause it to wheel to the right or left, by the same commands and the same means; but he should previously caution the battalion that it is to continue the march.

85. A battalion in line of battle will break into column by company to the left, according to the same principles and by inverse means; the covering sergeant of each company will conduct the marching flank, and the left guides will place themselves on the left of their respective companies at the command *forward*.

86. When a battalion has to prolong itself in column towards the right or left, or has to direct its march in column perpendicularly or diagonally in front, or in rear of either flank, the colonel will cause it to break by company to the right or left, as has just been prescribed; but when the line breaks to the right, in order to march towards the left, or the reverse, the colonel will command: *Break to the right to march to the left*, or *break to the left to march to the right*, before giving the command, *by company, right* (or *left*) *wheel.* As soon as the battalion is broken, the lieutenant

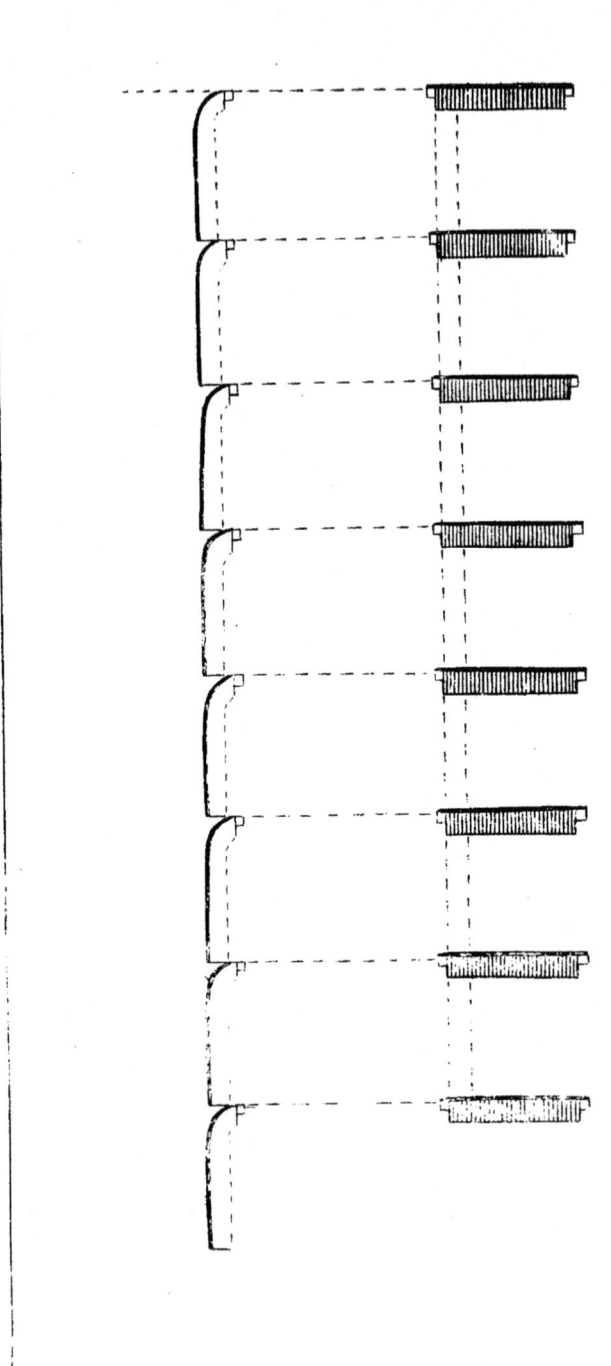

SCHOOL OF THE BATTALION—PART II. 23

colonel will place a marker abreast with the right guide of the leading company. The instant the column is put in motion, this company will wheel to the left (or right) march ten paces to the front without changing the guide, and wheel again to the left (or right.) The second wheel being completed, the captain will immediately command *guide left* (or *right.*) The guide of this company will march in a direction parallel to the guides of the column. The lieutenant colonel will be careful to place a second marker at the point where the first company is to change direction the second time.

ARTICLE SECOND.

To break to the rear, by the right or left, into column, and to advance or retire by the right or left of companies.

87. When the colonel shall wish to cause the battalion to break to the rear, by the right, into column by company, he will command:

1. *By the right of companies to the rear into column.* 2. *Battalion right*—FACE. 3. MARCH (or *double quick*—MARCH).

88. At the first command, each captain will place himself before the centre of his company, and caution it to face to the right; the covering sergeants will step into the front rank.

89. At the second command, the battalion will face to the right; each captain will hasten to the right of his company, and break two files to the rear; the first file will break the whole depth of the two ranks; the second file less; which being executed, the captain will place himself so that his breast may touch lightly the left arm of the front rank man of the last file in the company next on the right of his own. The captain of the right company will place himself as if there were a company on his right, and will align himself on the other captains. The covering sergeant of each company will break to the rear with the right files, and place himself before the front rank of the first file, to conduct him.

90. At the command *march*, the first file of each company will wheel to the right; the covering sergeant, placed before this file, will conduct it perpendicularly to the rear. The other files will come successively to wheel on the same spot. The captains will stand fast, see their companies file past, and at the instant the last file shall have wheeled, each captain will command:

1. *Such company.* 2. Halt. 3. Front. 4. *Left*—Dress.

91. At the instant the company faces to the front, its left guide will place himself so that his left arm may touch lightly the breast of his captain.

92. At the fourth command, the company will align itself on its left guide, the captain so direct-

ing it, that the new alignment may be perpendicular to that which the company had occupied in line of battle, and, the better to judge this, he will step back two paces from the flank.

93. The company being aligned, the captain will command: FRONT, and take his place before its centre.

94. The battalion marching in line of battle, when the colonel shall wish to break into column by company, to the rear, by the right, he will command:

1. *By the right of companies to the rear into column.* 2. *Battalion, by the right flank.* 3. MARCH (or *double quick*—MARCH).

95. At the first command, each captain will step briskly in front of the centre of his company, and caution it to face *by the right flank*.

96. At the command *march*, the battalion will face to the right; each captain will move rapidly to the right of his company and cause it to break to the right; the first file of each company will wheel to the right, and the covering sergeant placed in front of this file will conduct it perpendicularly to the rear; the other files will wheel successively at the same place as the first. The captains will see their companies file past them; when the last files have wheeled, the colonel will command:

3. *Battalion, by the left flank*—MARCH.
4 *Guide left.*

97. At the command *march*, the companies will face to the left, and march in column in the new direction. The captains will place themselves in front of the centres of their respective companies. At the fourth command, the guides will conform to the principles of the march in column; the leading one will move in the direction indicated to him by the lieutenant colonel. The men will take the touch of elbows to the left.

98. To break to the rear by the left, the colonel will give the same commands as in the case of breaking to the rear by the right, substituting the indication *left*, for that of *right*.

99. The movement will be executed according to the same principles. Each captain will hasten to the left of his company, cause the first two files to break to the rear, and then place his breast against the right file of the company next on the left of his own, in the manner prescribed above.

100. As soon as the two files break to the rear, the left guide of each company will place himself before the front rank man of the headmost file, to conduct him.

101. The instant the companies face to the front, the right guide of each will place himself so that his right arm may lightly touch the breast of his captain.

102. The battalion may be broken by division to the rear, by the right or left, in like manner; in this case, the indication *divisions* will be substituted, in the first command, for that of *companies;* the chiefs of division will conform themselves to what is prescribed for the chiefs of company. The junior captain in each division will place himself,

when the division faces to a flank, by the side of the covering sergeant of the left company, who steps into the front rank.

103. If there be an odd number of companies, and the battalion breaks by division to the rear, whether by the right or left, the captain of the left company will conform to what is prescribed No. 77.

104. This manner of breaking into column being at once the most prompt and regular, will be preferred on actual service, unless there be some particular reason for breaking to the front.

105. If the battalion be in line and at a halt, and the colonel should wish to advance or retire by the right of companies, he will command:

1. *By the right of companies to the front* (or *rear*).
2. *Battalion, right*—FACE. 3. MARCH (or *double quick*—MARCH). 4. *Guide right,* (*left*) *or* (*centre*).

106. At the first command, each captain will move rapidly two paces in front of the centre of his company, and caution it to face to the right; the covering sergeants will replace the captains in the front rank.

107. At the second command, the battalion will face to the right, and each captain moving quickly to the right of his company will cause files to break to the front, according to the principles indicated No. 89.

108. At the command *march*, each captain placing himself on the left of his leading guide will conduct his company perpendicularly to the

original line. At the fourth command, the guide of each company will dress to the right, left, or centre, according to the indication given, taking care to preserve accurately his distance.

109. If the colonel should wish to move to the front, or rear, by the left of companies, the movement will be executed by the same means and the same commands, substituting *left* for *right*.

110. If the battalion be in march, and the colonel should wish to advance or retire by the right of companies, he will command:

1. *By the right of companies to the front* (or *rear*).
2. *Battalion, by the right flank.* 3. MARCH (or *double quick*—MARCH). 4. *Guide right* (*left*) or (*centre*).

111. Which will be executed according to the principles and means prescribed Nos. 95 and following, and 106 and following. At the first command, the color and general guides will take their places as in column.

112. If the colonel should wish to advance or retire by the left of companies, the movement will be executed by the same means and the same commands, substituting *left* for *right*.

113. If the battalion be advancing by the right or left of companies, and the colonel should wish to form line to the front, he will command:

1. *By companies into line.* 2. MARCH (or *double quick*—MARCH). 3. *Guide centre.*

114. At the command *march*, briskly repeated by the captains, each company will be formed into line, as prescribed in the school of the company, No. 154.

115. At the third command, the color and general guides will move rapidly to their places in line, as will be hereinafter prescribed No. 405.

116. If the battalion be retiring by the right or left of companies, and the colonel should wish to form line facing the enemy, he will first cause the companies to face about while marching, and immediately form in line by the commands and means prescribed Nos. 113 and following.

Article Third.

To ploy the battalion into close column.

117. This movement may be executed by company or by division, on the right or left subdivision, or on any other subdivision, right or left in front.

118. The examples in this school will suppose the presence of four divisions, with directions for an odd company; but what will be prescribed for four, will serve equally for two, three or five divisions.

119. To ploy the battalion into close column by division in rear of the first, the colonel will command:

3 *

1. *Close column, by division.* 2. *On the first division, right in front.* 3. *Battalion, right*—Face. 4. March (or *double quick*—March).

120. At the second command, all the chiefs of division will place themselves before the centres of their divisions; the chief of the first will caution it to stand fast; the chiefs of the three others will remind them that they will have to face to the right, and the covering sergeant of the right company of each division will replace his captain in the front rank, as soon as the latter steps out.

121. At the third command, the last three divisions will face to the right; the chief of each division will hasten to its right, and cause files to be broken to the rear, as indicated No. 89; the right guide will break at the same time, and place himself before the front rank man of the first file, to conduct him, and each chief of division will place himself by the side of this guide.

122. The moment these divisions face to the right, the junior captain in each will place himself on the left of the covering sergeant of the left company, who will place himself in the front rank. *This rule is general for all the ployments by division.*

123. At the command *march*, the chief of the first division will add, *guide left;* at this, its left guide will place himself on its left, as soon as the movement of the second division may permit, and the file closers will advance one pace upon the rear rank.

124. All the other divisions, each conducted by its chief, will step off together, to take their places in the column; the second will gain, in wheeling by file to the rear, the space of six paces, which ought to separate its guide from the guide of the first division, and so direct its march as to enter the column on a line parallel to this division; the third and fourth divisions will direct themselves diagonally towards, but a little in rear of, the points at which they ought, respectively, to enter the column; at six paces from the left flank of the column, the head of each of these divisions will incline a little to the left, in order to enter the column as has just been prescribed for the second, taking care also to leave the distance of six paces between its guide and the guide of the preceding division. At the moment the divisions put themselves in march to enter the column, the file closers of each will incline to the left, so as to bring themselves to the distance of a pace from the rear rank.

125. Each chief of these three divisions will conduct his division till he shall be up with the guide of the directing one; the chief will then himself halt, see his division file past, and halt it the instant the last file shall have passed, commanding: 1. *Such division;* 2. HALT; 3. FRONT: 4. *Left*—DRESS.

126. At the second command, the division will halt; the left guide will place himself promptly on the direction, six paces from the guide which precedes him, in order that, the column being formed, the divisions may be separated the distance of four paces.

127. At the third command, the division will face to the front; at the fourth, it will be aligned by its chief, who will place himself two paces outside of his guide, and direct the alignment so that his division may be parallel to that which precedes — which being done, he will command, FRONT and place himself before the centre of his division.

128. If any division, after the command *front*, be not at its proper distance, and this can only happen through the negligence of its chief, such division will remain in its place, in order that the fault may not be propagated.

129. The colonel will superintend the execution of the movement, and cause the prescribed principles to be observed.

130. The lieutenant colonel, placing himself in succession in rear of the left guides, will assure them on the direction as they arrive, and then move to his place outside of the left flank of the column six paces from, and abreast with, the first division. In assuring the guides on the direction, he will be a mere observer, unless one or more should fail to cover exactly the guide or guides already established. *This rule is general.*

131. The major will follow the movement abreast with the left of the fourth division, and afterwards take his position outside of the left flank of the column, six paces from, and abreast with, this division.

132. To ploy the battalion in front of the first division, the colonel will give the same commands, substituting the indication *left* for that of *right* in front.

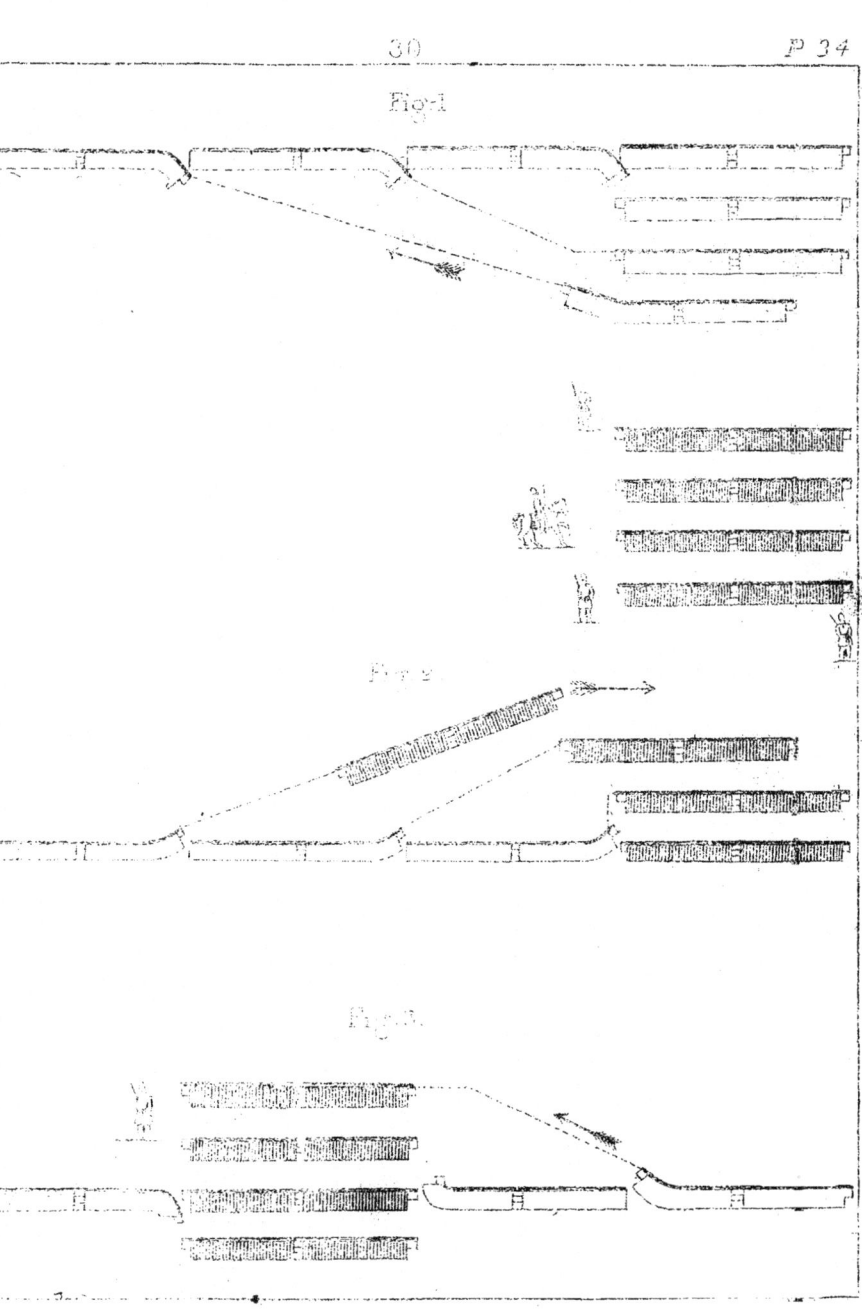

133. At the second and third commands, the chiefs of division and the junior captains will conform themselves to what is prescribed, Nos. 120, 121, 122; but the chiefs of the last three divisions, instead of causing the first two files to break to the rear, will cause them to break to the front.

134. At the fourth command, the chief of the first division will add: *Guide right.*

135. The three other divisions will step off together to take their places in the column in front of the directing division; each will direct itself as prescribed, No. 124, and will enter in such manner that, when halted, its guide may find himself six paces from the guide of the division next previously established in the column.

136. Each chief of these divisions will conduct his division, till his right guide shall be nearly up with the guide of the directing one; he will then halt his division, and cause it to face to the front; at the instant it halts, its right guide will face to the rear, place himself six paces from the preceding guide, and cover him exactly — which being done, the chief will align his division by the right.

137. The lieutenant colonel, placed in front of the right guide of the first division, will assure the guides on the direction as they successively arrive, and then move outside of the right flank of the column, to a point six paces from, and abreast with, the fourth division, now in front.

138. The major will conform himself to what is prescribed, No. 131, and then move outside of the right flank of the column, six paces from, and abreast with, the first division, now in the rear.

c

139. The movement being ended, the **colonel** will command:

Guides, about—F<small>ACE</small>.

140. At this, the guides, who are faced to the rear, will face to the front.

141. To ploy the battalion in rear, or in front of the fourth division, the colonel will command:

1. *Close column by division.* 2. *On the fourth division, left* (or *right*) *in front.* 3. *Battalion, left*—F<small>ACE</small>. 4. M<small>ARCH</small> (*or double quick*—M<small>ARCH</small>).

142. These movements will be executed according to the principles of those which precede, but by inverse means: the fourth division on which the battalion ploys will stand fast; the instant the movement commences, its chief will command, *guide right* (or *left*).

143. The foregoing examples embrace all the principles: thus, when the colonel shall wish to ploy the battalion on an interior division, he will command:

1. *Close column by division.* 2. *On such division, right* (or *left*) *in front.* 3. *Battalion inwards*—F<small>ACE</small>. 4. M<small>ARCH</small> (*or double quick*—M<small>ARCH</small>).

144. The instant the movement commences, the chief of the directing division will command, *guide left* (or *right*).

145. The divisions which, in the order in battle,

SCHOOL OF THE BATTALION—PART II. 35

are to the right of the directing division, will face to the left; those which are to the left, will face to the right.

146. If the right is to be in front, the right divisions will ploy in front of the directing division, and the left in its rear; the reverse, if the left is to be in front. And in all the foregoing suppositions, the division or divisions contiguous to the directing one, in wheeling by file to the front or rear, will gain the space of six paces, which ought to separate their guides from the guide of the directing division.

147. In all the ployments on an interior division, the lieutenant colonel will assure the positions of the guides in front, and the major those in rear of the directing division.

148. If the battalion be in march, instead of at a halt, the movement will be executed by combining the two gaits of quick and double quick time, and always in rear of one of the flank divisions.

149. The battalion being in march, to ploy it in rear of the first division, the colonel will command:

1. *Close column by division.* 2. *On the first division.* 3. *Battalion — by the right flank.* 4. *Double quick*—March.

150. At the second command, each chief of division will move rapidly before the centre of his division and caution it to face to the right.

151. The chief of the first division will caution it to continue to march to the front, and he will command: *Quick march.*

152. At the command *march*, the chief of the first division will command: *Guide left*. At this, the left guide will move to the left flank of the division and direct himself on the point indicated.

153. The three other divisions will face to the right and move off in double quick time, breaking to the right to take their places in column; each chief of division will move rapidly to the right of his division in order to conduct it. The files will be careful to preserve their distances, and to march with a uniform and decided step. The color-bearer and general guides will retake their places in the ranks.

154. The second division will immediately enter the column, marching parallel to the first division; its chief will allow it to file past him, and when the last file is abreast of him, will command: 1. *Second division, by the left flank*—March. 2. *Guide left*, and place himself in front of the centre of his division.

155. At the command *march*, the division will face to the left; at the second command, the left guide will march in the trace of the left guide of the first division; the men will take the touch of elbows to the left. When the second division has closed to its proper distance, its chief will command: *Quick time*—March. This division will then change its step to quick time.

156. The chiefs of the third and fourth divisions will execute their movements according to the same principles, taking care to gain as much ground as possible towards the head of the column.

157. If the battalion had been previously marching in line at double quick time, when the fourth

division shall have gained its distance, the colonel will command: *Double quick*—MARCH.

158. In this movement, the lieutenant colonel will move rapidly to the side of the leading guide, give him a point of direction, and then follow the movements of the first division. The major will follow the movement abreast with the left of the fourth division.

Remarks on ploying the battalion into column.

159. The battalion may be ployed into column at full, or half distance, on the same principles, and by the same commands, substituting for the first command: *Column at full* (or *half*) *distance by division.*

160. In the ployments and movements in column, when the subdivisions execute the movements successively, such as — to take or close distances; to change direction by the flank of subdivisions, each chief of subdivision will cause his men to support arms after having aligned it and commanded, FRONT.

PART THIRD.

ARTICLE FIRST.

To march in column at full distance.

161. When the colonel shall wish to put the column in march, he will indicate to the leading guide two distinct objects in front, on the line which the guide ought to follow. This guide will

immediately put his shoulders in a square with that line, take the more distant object as the point of direction, and the nearer one as the intermediate point.

162. If only a single prominent object present itself in the direction the guide has to follow, he will face to it as before, and immediately endeavor to catch on the ground some intermediate point, by which to give steadiness to his march on the point of direction.

163. There being no prominent object to serve as the point of direction, the colonel will despatch the lieutenant colonel or adjutant to place himself forty paces in advance, facing the column, and by a sign of the sword establish him on the direction he may wish to give to the leading guide; that officer being thus placed, this guide will take him as the point of direction, conforming himself to what is prescribed in the school of the company, No. 87.

164. These dispositions being made, the colonel will command:

1. *Column forward.* 2. *Guide left* (or *right.*) 3. March (or *double quick*—March).

165. At the command *march*, briskly repeated by the chiefs of subdivision, the column will put itself in march, conforming to what is prescribed in the school of the company No. 200 and following.

166. The leading guide may always maintain himself correctly on the direction by keeping steadily in view the two points indicated to him,

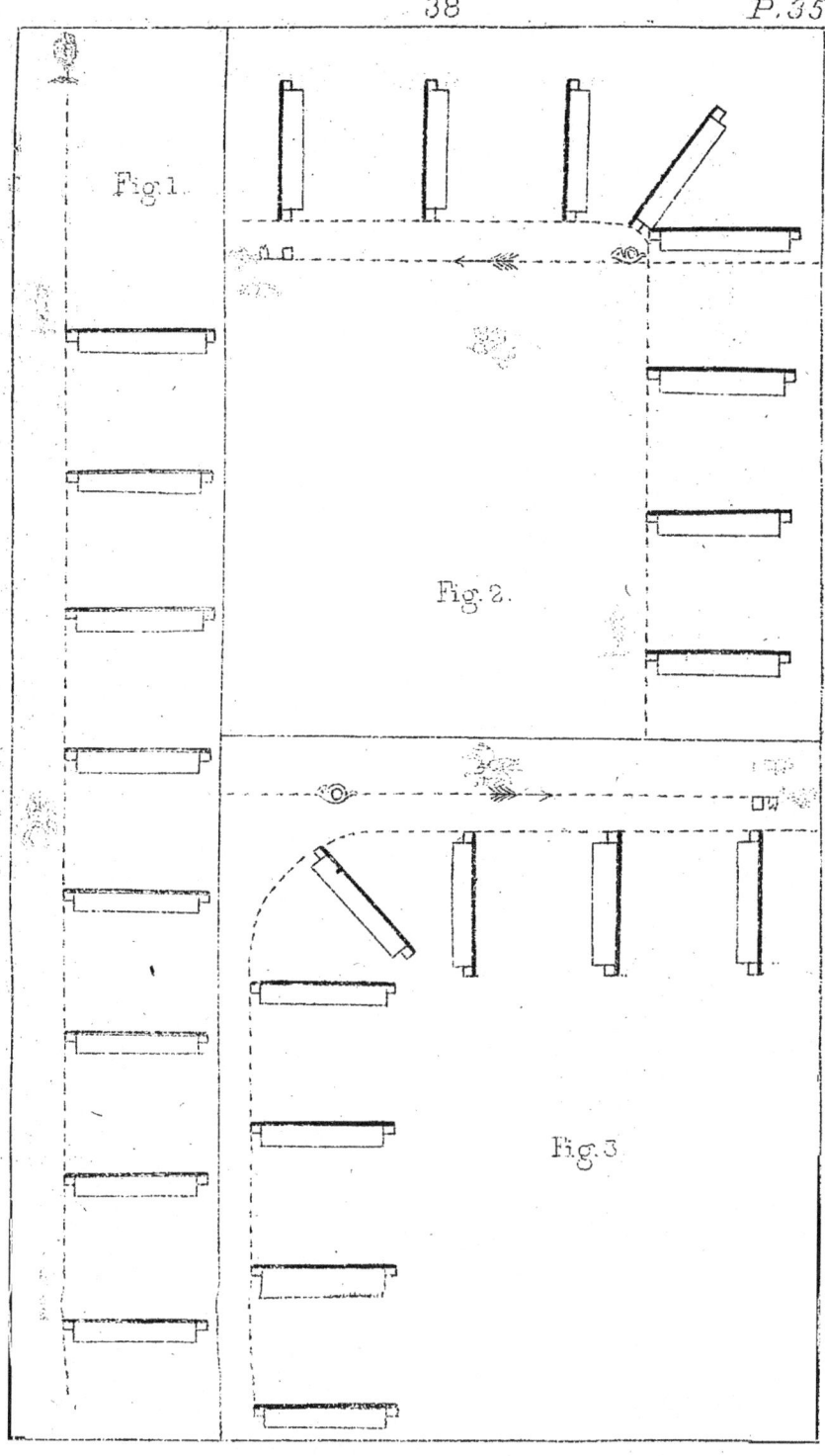

or chosen by himself; if these points have a certain elevation, he may be assured he is on the true direction, when the nearer masks the more distant point.

167. The following guides will preserve with exactness both step and distance; each will march in the trace of the guide who immediately precedes him, without occupying himself with the general direction.

168. The lieutenant colonel will hold himself, habitually, abreast with the leading guide, to see that he does not deviate from the direction, and will observe, also, that the next guide marches exactly in the trace of the first.

169. The major will generally be abreast with the last subdivision; he will see that each guide marches exactly in the trace of the one immediately preceding; if either deviate from the direction, the major will promptly rectify the error, and prevent its being propagated; but he need not interfere, in this way, unless the deviation has become sensible, or material.

170. The column being in march, the colonel will frequently cause the *about* to be executed while marching; to this effect, he will command:

1. *Battalion, right about.* 2. MARCH.
3. *Guide right.*

171. At the second command, the companies will face to the right about, and the column will then march forward in an opposite direction; the chiefs of subdivision will remain behind the front

rank, the file closers in front of the rear rank, and the guides will place themselves in the same rank. The lieutenant colonel will remain abreast of the first division, now in rear; the major will give a point of direction to the leading guide, and march abreast of him.

172. The colonel will hold himself habitually on the directing flank; he will look to the step and to the distances, and see that all the principles prescribed for the march in column, school of the company, are observed.

173. These means, which the practice in that school ought to have rendered familiar, will give sufficient exactness to the direction of the column, and also enable it to form *forward* or *faced the rear, on the right*, or *on the left*, into line of battle, and *to close in mass.*

174. But when a column, arriving in front, or in rear of the line of battle, or, rather, on one of the extremities of that line, has to prolong itself on it, in order to form *to the left* or *to the right* into line of battle, then, as it is essential, to prevent the column from cutting the line, or sensibly deviating from it, other means, as follows, will be employed.

The column arriving in front of the line of battle, to prolong it on this line.

175. If the column right in front arrive in front of the line of battle, as it should cross it and find itself four paces beyond it after having changed direction, the colonel will cause to be placed, in advance, a marker on the line to indicate the point

at which the column ought to cross it, and another marker to indicate the point where the first subdivision should commence to wheel; he will be so placed that when the wheel is executed, the left guide will find himself four paces within the line of battle. The chief of the leading subdivision, when the head of the column shall have arrived near the line, will take the guide to the right, and this guide will immediately direct himself on the second marker. On arriving abreast of him, this subdivision will be wheeled to the left, and when the wheel is completed, the guide will be changed again to the left; this guide will then march parallel to the line of battle by the means to be hereinafter indicated.

176. The instant the first subdivision wheels, the right general guide, who, by a caution from the lieutenant colonel, will before have placed himself on the line of battle at the point where the column crosses it, and who will have faced to the two points of direction in his front, indicated by the colonel, will march forward correctly on the prolongation of those points.

177. The color-bearer will place himself in like manner on the line of battle; and, at the instant the color subdivision wheels, he will prolong his march on that line, abreast with this subdivision, taking care to carry the color-lance before the centre of his person, and to maintain himself exactly in the direction of the general guide who precedes him, and the point of direction in front which will have been indicated to him.

178. Finally, the left general guide will place himself in the same manner on the line of battle;

and, at the instant the last subdivision of the battalion wheels, he will march correctly in the direction of the colour-bearer, and the other general guide.

179. The guide of the first subdivision will march steadily abreast with the right general guide, and about four paces to his right; each of the guides of the following subdivisions will march in the trace of the guide who immediately precedes him, as prescribed, No. 167.

180. The colonel, placed outside of the general guides, will see that the column marches nearly parallel to, and about four paces within these guides.

181. The lieutenant colonel and major will look to the direction of the general guides, and to this end, place themselves sometimes in rear of the color-bearer, or the left general guide.

182. If the column be composed of several battalions, the general guides of each will successively place themselves on the line of battle to prolong their march on this line, as the leading subdivision, that of the color, and the one in the rear of their battalion, shall wheel into the new direction; these guides will conform themselves respectively, as will also the colonel, lieutenant colonel, and major, to what is prescribed above for those of the leading battalion.

183. In the case of several battalions, the lieutenant colonel of each will maintain steadily the guide of his leading subdivision about four paces within the line of general guides, even should the last subdivisions of the battalion immediately preceding deviate from the parallelism, in order that

the false direction of one battalion may not influence that of the battalions which follow.

The column arriving behind the line of battle, to prolong it on this line.

184. If the column, right in front, arrive behind the line of battle, as it ought to find itself four paces within this line, after having changed direction, the colonel will cause a marker to be placed at the point where, according to that condition, the first subdivision ought to commence wheeling. Another marker will be established on the line of battle, to indicate the point at which the general guides ought, in succession, to begin to prolong themselves on that line; he will be so placed that each subdivision, having finished its wheel, may find itself nearly in a line with this marker.

185. At the instant the first subdivision, after having wheeled to the right, begins to prolong itself, parallelly to the line of battle, the leading general guide, placed in advance on that line, will direct himself on the two points taken in his front; the color-bearer and the other general guide will successively place themselves on the same line the instant that their respective subdivisions shall have finished their wheel.

186. If the column be composed of several battalions, the general guides of the following battalions will successively execute what has been just prescribed for those of the leading battalion, and the whole will conform themselves, as well as the guides of subdivisions, and the field officers of the

several battalions, to what is indicated, above, for a column arriving in front of the line of battle.

187. In a column, left in front, arriving in front or in rear of the line of battle, these movements will be executed on the same principles, and by inverse means.

The column arriving on the right or the left of the line of battle, to prolong it on this line.

188. If the column, instead of arriving in front or in rear of the line of battle, arrive on its right or left, and if it have to prolong itself on that line, in order afterwards to form to the left or right into line of battle, the colonel will bring the color and general guides on the flank of the column by the command *color and general guides on the line:* and these guides will prolong themselves on the line of battle, conforming to what is prescribed above.

Manner of prolonging a line of battle by markers.

189. When a column prolongs itself on the line of battle, it being all-important that the general guides march correctly on that line, it becomes necessary that colonels, lieutenant colonels, and majors, whose duty it is to maintain the true direction, should be able to see, as far as practicable, the two objects, on which the march of the general guides ought to be directed; consequently, when no prominent objects present themselves in the desired direction, the chief of the column will supply the want of them in advance by aids-de-

camp, or other mounted officers, and in such number as may be necessary.

190. Three such officers may prolong a line as far as may be desired in the following manner: they will place themselves in advance on the line of battle, the first at the point where the head of the column ought to enter; the second, three or four hundred paces behind the first, and the third, a like distance behind the second. The first of these officers will remain in position till the leading general guide shall have entered on the line of battle, and then, at a gallop, place himself at a convenient distance behind the third. The second will do the like in respect to the first, when the head of the column shall be near him, and so on in continuation. These officers, without dismounting, will face to the column, and cover each other accurately in file. It will be on them that the general guides will steadily direct their march, and it will be so much the more easy for the latter to maintain themselves on the direction, as they will always be able to see the mounted officers over the heads of the preceding guides; thus the deviation from the direction, by one or more general guides, need not mislead those who follow.

191. A single mounted officer may suffice to assure the direction of a column, when the point of direction towards which it marches is very distinct. In this case, that officer will place himself on the line of battle within that point, and beyond the one at which the head of the column will halt, and remain in position till the column halts; serving thus as the intermediate point for giving steadiness to the march of the general guides.

192. For a column of one or two battalions, markers on foot will suffice to indicate the line to be followed by the general guides.

Remarks on the march in column.

193. Although the uncadenced step be that of columns in route marches, and also that which ought to be habitually employed in the *Evolutions of the Line*, because it leaves the men more at ease, and, consequently, is better adapted to movements on a large scale and to difficult grounds, nevertheless, as it is of paramount importance to confirm soldiers in the measure and the movement of the cadenced pace, the route step will be but little practised in the exercises by battalion, except in going to, and returning from, the ground of instruction, and for teaching the mechanism and movements of columns in route.

194. It is highly essential to the regularity of the march in column that each guide follow exactly in the trace of the one immediately preceding, without occupying his attention with the general direction of the guides. If this principle be steadily observed, the guides will find themselves aligned, provided that the leading one march exactly in the direction indicated to him; and even should obstacles in his way force him into a momentary deviation, the direction of the column would not necessarily be changed; whereas, if the following guides endeavor to conform themselves at once to all the movements of the leading one, in order to cover him in file, such endeavors would necessarily cause corresponding fluctuations

47

in the column, from right to left, and from left to right, and render the preservation of distances extremely difficult.

195. As a consequence of the principle, that *each guide shall exactly follow in the trace of the one who immediately precedes*, if, pending the march of the column, the colonel shall give a new point of direction, too near to the first to require a formal change of direction, the leading guide, advancing the one or other shoulder, will immediately direct himself on this point; the other guides will only conform themselves to this movement as each arrives at the point at which the first had executed it. Each subdivision will conform itself to the movement of its guide, the men insensibly lengthening or shortening the step, and advancing or refusing (throwing back) the shoulder opposite to the guide, but without losing the touch of the elbow towards his side.

196. The column, by company, being in march, the colonel will cause it to diminish front by platoon, from front to rear, at once, and to increase front by platoon in like manner, which movements will be commanded and executed as prescribed in the school of the company, Nos. 282 and 273 and following, changing the command *form company* to *form companies*. So may he increase and diminish, or diminish and increase front, according to the same principles and at once, by company, changing the command *form companies* to *form divisions*, and the command *break into platoons*, to *break into companies*. In this case, the companies and divisions will execute

what is prescribed for platoons and companies respectively.

197. The column being at a halt, if the colonel should wish to march it to the rear, and the distance to be gained be so inconsiderable as to render a countermarch a disproportionate loss of time, he will cause the column to face about, and then put it in march by the commands prescribed No. 164; the chiefs of the subdivisions will remain behind the front rank, the file closers before the rear rank, and the guides will step into the rear rank, now in front. In a column, by division, the junior captains, in the intervals between companies, will replace their covering sergeants in the rear rank, and these sergeants will step into the line of file closers in front of their intervals.

Article Second.

Column in route.

198. A column in route, like a column in manœuvre, ought never to have a depth greater than about the front it had occupied in the line of battle, less the front of a subdivision.

199. The observance of this principle requires no particular rule for a column in manœuvre; but, as a column in route may have hourly to pass narrow ways, bridges, or other defiles, rendering it necessary to diminish the front of subdivisions, it becomes important to give rules and means by which the column may, for any length of march,

SCHOOL OF THE BATTALION—PART III. 49

preserve the ease of the route step without elongation from front to rear.

200. A column in route will be habitually formed by company.

201. When a column in route shall arrive at a pass too narrow to receive the front of a company, the column will diminish front by platoon before entering. This movement will be executed successively, or by all the companies at once.

202. If, however, the defile be very short, and it may be passed by the diminution of a few files, it will be preferable to break to the rear the limited number of files.

203. The column being by platoon, and the want of space rendering a further diminution of front necessary, it will be diminished by section, if the platoons be of twelve or more files.

204. The column being by section, will continue to march by that front as long as the defile may permit.

205. If the platoons have less than twelve files, one or two files will be broken to the rear, according to the narrowing of the defile, and the route step continued as long as six files can march abreast.

206. What has just been explained for breaking files to the rear in a column by platoon, is equally applicable to a column by section.

207. If the defile be too narrow to permit six men to march abreast, the subdivisions will be marched successively by the flank, conforming to what is prescribed Nos. 314 and 315, school of the company.

208. The battalion marching by the flank, will

be formed into column, by section, by platoon, or by company, as soon as the breadth of the way may permit; the several movements which these formations include will be executed by the commands of the captains, as their companies successively clear the defile, observing the following rules.

209. As soon as the way is sufficiently broad to contain six men abreast, the captain will command:

1. *By section* (or *by platoon*) *into line.* 2. MARCH.

210. At the command *march*, the subdivisions indicated will form themselves into line; the files which have not been able to enter, will follow (by the flank) the last four files of their subdivision which have entered into line.

211. The column marching in this order, the files in rear will be caused to enter into line as the increased breadth of the way may permit.

212. The column marching by section or by platoon, platoons or companies will be formed as soon as the breadth of the way may permit.

213. The leading subdivision will follow the windings of the pass or defile; the following subdivisions will not occupy themselves with the direction, but all, in succession, pass over the trace of the subdivisions which precede them respectively. The men will not seek to avoid the bad parts of the way, but pass, as far as practicable, each in the direction of his file.

214. Changes of direction will always be made without command; if the change be important, a

SCHOOL OF THE BATTALION—PART III. 51

caution merely from the respective chiefs to their subdivisions will suffice, and the rear rank, as well as the files broken to the rear, will execute successively the movement where the front rank had executed it.

215. The colonel will hold himself at the head of the battalion; he will regulate the step of the leading subdivision, and indicate to its chief the instant for executing the various movements which the nature of the route may render necessary.

216. If the column be composed of several battalions, each will conform itself, in its turn, to what shall have been commanded for the leading battalion, observing to execute each movement at the same place, and in the same manner.

217. Finally, to render the mechanism of all those movements familiar to the troops, and to habituate them to march in the route step without elongating the column, commanders will generally cause their battalions to march in this step, going to, and returning from, fields of exercise. Each will occasionally conduct his battalion through narrow passes, in order to make it perceive the utility of the principles prescribed above; and he will several times, in every course of instruction, march it in the route step, and cause to be executed, sometimes at once, and sometimes successively, the divers movements which have just been indicated.

General remarks on the column in route.

218. The lesson relative to the column in route is, by its frequent application, one of the most important that can be given to troops. If it be not well taught and established on right principles, it will happen that the rear of the column in route will be obliged to run, to regain distances, or that the front will be forced to halt till the rear shall have accomplished that object; thus rendering the march greatly slower, or greatly more fatiguing, generally both, than if it were executed according to rule.

219. The ordinary progress of a column in route ought to be, on good roads or good grounds, at the rate of one hundred and ten paces in a minute. This rate may be easily maintained by columns of almost any depth; but over bad roads, ploughed fields, loose sands, or mountainous districts, the progress cannot be so great, and must therefore be regulated according to circumstances.

220. The most certain means of marching well in route, is to preserve always a regular and equal movement, and, if obstacles oblige one or more subdivisions to slacken or to shorten the step, to cause the primitive rate of march to be resumed the moment the difficulties are passed.

221. A subdivision ought never to take *more* than the prescribed distance from the subdivision immediately preceding; but it is sometimes necessary to *lessen* that distance.

222. Thus: the head of the column encounters an obstacle which obliges it to relax its march; all

the following subdivisions will preserve the habitual step, and close up in mass, if necessary, on the subdivision nearest to the obstacle. Distances will afterwards naturally be recovered as each subdivision shall successively have passed the obstacle. Nevertheless, if the difficulty be too great to be overcome by one subdivision, whilst the next is closing up, so that distances cannot afterwards be recovered without running, the chief of the column will halt the leading subdivision beyond the obstacle, at a distance sufficient to contain the whole column in mass. He will then put the column in march, the subdivisions taking distances by the head, observing to commence the movement in time, so that the last subdivision may not be obliged to halt, after having cleared the obstacle.

223. When the chief of a column shall wish to change the rate of march, he will cause the leading battalion to quicken or to relax the step insensibly, and send orders to the other battalions each to regulate itself by that which precedes it.

224. The column being composed of several battalions, the general-in-chief will always leave an aid-de-camp with its rear to bring him prompt information if it find a difficulty in following.

225. Subdivisions ought always to step out well in obliquing, both in breaking and forming companies or platoons. When either is done in succession, it is highly important that no subdivision slacken or shorten the step whilst that which precedes it is engaged in the movement. The observance of this principle can alone prevent an elongation of the column.

226. If the battalion, marching by the flank,

encounter a pass so narrow as to oblige it to defile with a front of two men, the colonel will order support arms, take the cadenced step, and undouble the files, which will be executed as prescribed in the school of the company, No. 326; the files will double again as soon as the breadth of the way will permit.

227. If the defile be only sufficient to receive a front of one man, the colonel will cause the men to pass one at a time. The men of the same file should follow each other in their order as closely as possible, and without loss of time. As soon as the defile permits a front of two or four men, the battalion will be re-formed into two or four ranks, and will march in this order until there be space to form platoons or sections, as indicated No. 209.

228. In both cases, just supposed, the head of the battalion, after having passed the defile, will march till sufficient space be left to contain the whole of the subdivisions in mass; afterwards it will be put in march by the means indicated No. 222.

229. When a command has to move rapidly over a given distance, the movements prescribed in this article will be executed in double quick time; if the distance be long, the chief of the column will not allow the march at this gait to be continued for more than fifteen minutes; at the end of this time, he will order the ordinary route step to be marched for five minutes, and then again resume the double quick. If the ground be uneven, having considerable ascents and descents, he will reserve the double quick for those parts of the ground most favorable to this march.

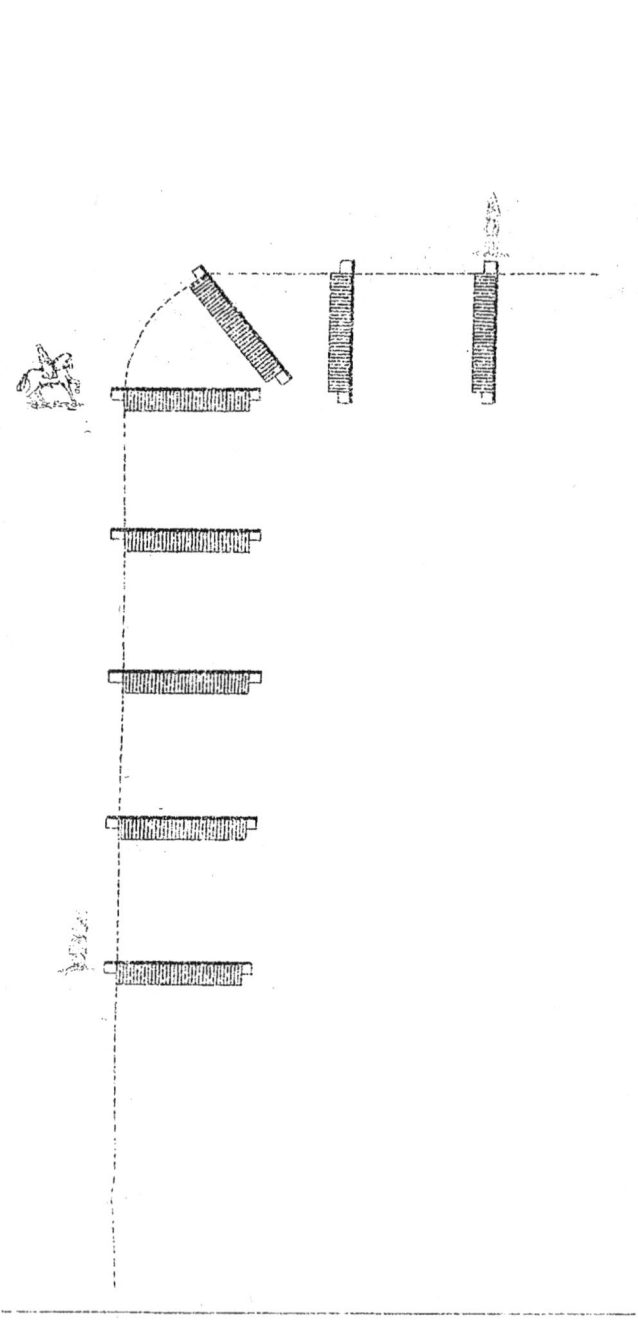

230. A column marching alternately in double quick time and the ordinary route step, in the manner stated, can easily accomplish very long distances in a very short space of time; but when the distance to be passed over be not greater than two miles, it ought to be accomplished, when the ground is favorable, without changing the rate of march.

Article Third.

To change direction in column at full distance.

231. The column being in march in the cadenced step, when the colonel shall wish to cause it to change direction, he will go to the point at which the change ought to be commenced, and establish a marker there, presenting the breast to the flank of the column; this marker, no matter to which side the change of direction is to be made, will be posted on the opposite side, and he will remain in position till the last subdivision of the battalion shall have passed. The leading subdivision being within a few paces of the marker, the colonel will command:

Head of column to the left (or *right*).

232. At this, the chief of the leading subdivision will immediately take the guide on the side opposite the change of direction, if not already there. This guide will direct himself so as to graze the breast of the marker; arrived at this point, the chief will cause his subdivision to

change direction by the commands and according to the principles prescribed in the school of the company. When the wheel is completed, the chief of this subdivision will retake the guide, if changed, on the side of the primitive direction.

233. The chief of each succeeding subdivision, as well as the guides, will conform to what has just been explained for the leading subdivision.

235. The colonel will carefully see that the guide of each subdivision, in wheeling, does not throw himself without or within, but passes over all the points of the arc of the circle, which he ought to describe.

233. As often as no distinct object presents itself in the new direction, the lieutenant colonel will place himself upon it in advance, at the distance of thirty or forty paces from the marker, and be assured in this direction by the colonel; the leading guide will take, the moment he shall have changed direction, two points on the ground in the straight line which, drawn from himself, would pass between the heels of the lieutenant colonel, taking, afterwards, new points as he advances.

236. The major will see that the guides direct themselves on the marker posted at the point of change, so as to graze his breast.

237. If the column be composed of several battalions, the lieutenant colonel of the second, will cause the marker of the first battalion, to be replaced as soon as the last subdivision of this battalion shall have passed; this disposition will be observed by battalion after battalion, to the rear of the column.

Remarks.

238. It has been demonstrated, school of the company, how important it is, *first*, that each subdivision execute its change of direction precisely at the point where the leading one had changed, and that it arrive in a square with the direction; *second*, that the wheeling point ought, always, to be cleared in time, in order that the subdivision engaged in the wheel may not arrest the movement of the following one. The deeper the column, the more rigorously ought these principles to be observed; because, a fault that would be but slight in a column of a single battalion, would cause much embarrassment in one of great depth.

ARTICLE FOURTH.

To halt the column.

239. The column being in march, when the colonel shall wish to halt it, he will command:

1. *Column.* 2. HALT.

240. At the second command, briskly repeated by the captains, the column will halt; no guide will stir, though he may have lost his distance, or be out of the direction of the preceding guides.

241. The column being in march, in double quick time, will be halted by the same commands. At the command *halt*, the men will halt in their

places, and will themselves rectify their positions in the ranks.

242. The column being halted, when the colonel shall wish to form it into line of battle, he will move a little in front of the leading guide, and face to him; this guide and the following one will fix their eyes on the colonel, in order promptly to conform themselves to his directions.

243. If the colonel judge it not necessary to give a general direction to the guides, he will limit himself to rectifying the position of such as may be without, or within the direction, by the command *guide of* (such) *company,* or *guides of* (such) *companies, to the right,* (or *to the left;*) at this command, the guides designated will place themselves on the direction; the others will stand fast.

244. If, on the contrary, the colonel judge it necessary to give a general direction to the guides of the column, he will place the first two on the direction he shall have chosen, and command:

Guides, cover.

245. At this, the following guides will promptly place themselves on the direction covering the first two in file, and each precisely at a distance equal to the front of his company, from the guide immediately preceding; the lieutenant colonel will assure them in the direction, and the colonel will command:

Left, (or *right*)—Dress.

246. At this command, each company will incline to the right or left, and dress forward or backward, so as to bring the designated flank to rest on its guide; each captain will place himself two paces outside of his guide, promptly align his company parallelly with that which precedes, then command Front, and return to his place in column.

247. Finally, if the general guides march on the flank of the column, the colonel, having halted it, will place himself in rear of the color-bearer, to ascertain whether the leading general guide and the color-bearer be exactly on the direction of the two points in advance, and establish them on that direction if they be not already on it; the major will do the like, in respect to the general guide in the rear; which being executed, the colonel will command:

1. *Guides*—On the line.

248. At this command, the guide of each company of the directing flank will step promptly into the direction of the general guides, and face to the front. The lieutenant colonel, placed in front of, and facing to, the leading general guide, and the major, placed in rear of the rearmost one, will promptly align the company guides.

249. The colonel, having verified the direction of the guides, will command:

Left (or *right*)—Dress.

250. This will be executed as prescribed, No. 246.

Remarks.

251. The means indicated, No. 244, and following, for giving a general direction to the guides of a column, at full distance, will apply only to a column composed of two, or, at most, three battalions. If the number be more numerous, its chief will cause the colors and general guides of all the battalions to step out and place themselves on the direction which he may wish to give to the column, as is explained in the evolutions of the line.

Article Fifth.

To close the column to half distance, or in mass.

252. A column by co any being at full distance right in front, and at a halt, when the colonel shall wish to cause it to close to half distance, on the leading company, he will command:

1. *To half distance, close column.* 2. March (or *double quick*—March.)

253. At the first command, the captain of the leading company will caution it to stand fast.

254. At the command *march*, which will be repeated by all the captains, except the captain of the leading company, this company will stand fast, and its chief will align it by the left; the file closers will close one pace upon the rear rank.

255. All the other companies will continue to march, and as each in succession arrives at platoon distance from the one which precedes, its captain will halt it.

256. At the instant that each company halts, its guide will place himself on the direction of the guides who precede, and the captain will align the company by the left; the file closers will close one pace upon the rear rank.

257. No particular attention need be given to the general direction of the guides before they respectively halt; it will suffice if each follow in the trace of the one who precedes him.

258. The colonel, on the side of the guides, will superintend the execution of the movement, observing that the captains halt their companies exactly at platoon distance the one from the other.

259. The lieutenant colonel, a few paces in front, will face to the leading guide and assure the positions of the following guides as they successively place themselves on the direction.

260. The major will follow the movement abreast with the last guide.

261. If the column be in march, the colonel will cause it to close by the same commands.

262. If the column be marching in double quick time, at the first command, the captain of the leading company will command *quick time;* the chiefs of the other companies will caution them to continue their march.

263. At the command *march,* the leading company will march in quick, and the other companies in double quick time; and as each arrives at

platoon distance from the preceding one, its chief will cause it to march in quick time.

264. When the rearmost company shall have gained its distance, the colonel will command:

Double quick—MARCH.

265. When the colonel shall wish to halt the column and to cause it to close to half distance at the same time, he will notify the captain of the leading company of his intention, who at the command *march* will halt his company and align it by the left.

266. If the column be marching in quick time, and the colonel should not give the command *double quick*, the captain of the leading company will halt his company at the command *march*, and align it by the left. In the case, where the colonel adds the command *double quick*, the captains of companies will conform to what is prescribed No. 262, and the movement will be executed as indicated No. 263.

To close the column on the eighth, or rearmost company.

267. The column being at a halt, if instead of causing it to close to half distance on the first company, the colonel should wish to cause it to close on the eighth, he will command:

1. *On the eighth company, to half distance close column.* 2. *Battalion about*—FACE. 3. *Column forward.* 4. *Guide right.* 5. MARCH (or *double quick*—MARCH).

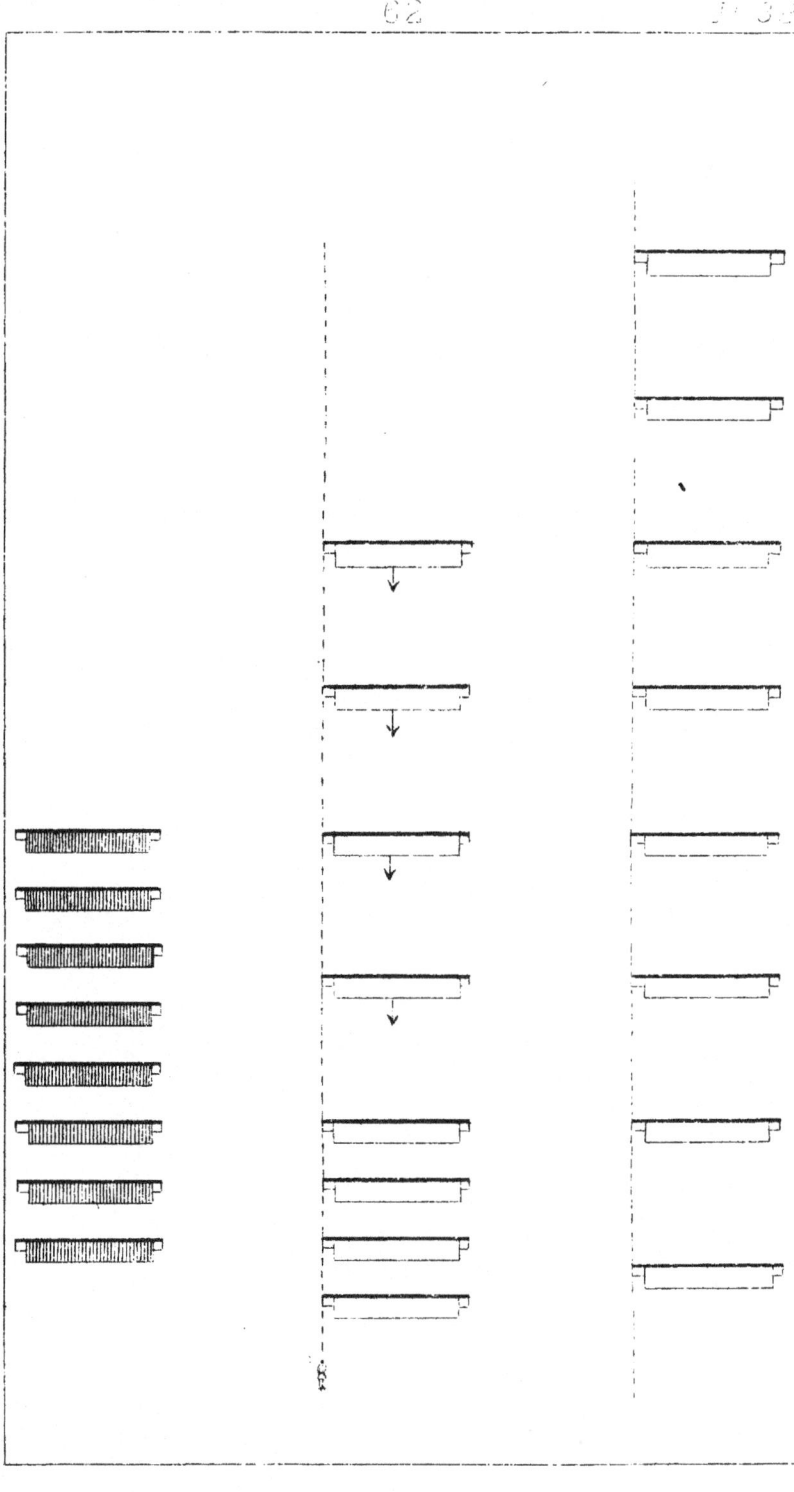

268. At the second command, all the companies except the eighth, will face about, and their guides will remain in the front rank, now the rear.

269. At the fourth command, all the captains will place themselves two paces outside of their companies on the directing flank.

270. At the command *march*, the eighth company will stand fast, and its captain will align it by the left, the other companies will put themselves in march, and, as each arrives at platoon distance from the one established before it, its captain will halt it and face it to the front. At the moment that each company halts, the left guide, remaining faced to the rear, will place himself promptly on the direction of the guides already established. Immediately after, the captain will align his company by the left, and the file closers will close one pace on the rear rank. If this movement be executed in double quick time, each captain, in turn, will halt, and command: *Such company, right about* —Halt. At this command, the company designated will face to the right about and halt.

271. All the companies being aligned, the colonel will cause the guides, who stand faced to the rear, to face about.

272. The lieutenant colonel, placing himself behind the rearmost guide, will assure successively the positions of the other guides, as prescribed No. 259; the major will remain abreast with the rearmost company.

273. The column being in march, when the colonel shall wish to close it on the eighth company, he will command:

1. *On the eighth company, to half distance, close column.* 2. *Battalion right about.* 3. March (or *double quick*—March.) 4. *Guide right.*

274. At the first command, the captain of the eighth company will caution his company that it will remain faced to the front; the captains of the other companies will caution their companies that they will have to face about.

275. At the command *march*, the captain of the eighth company will halt his company and align it by the left; the file closers will close one pace upon the rear rank.

276. The captains of the other companies, at the same command, will place themselves on the flank of the column; the subdivisions will face about, and as each arrives at platoon distance from the company immediately preceding it, its chief will face it to the front and halt it as prescribed No. 270. The instant each company halts, the guide on the directing flank, remaining faced to the rear, will quickly place himself on the direction of the guides already established. After which, the captain will align the company by the left, and the file closers will close one pace upon the rear rank.

277. The lieutenant colonel will follow the movement abreast of the first company. The major will place himself a few paces in rear of the guide of the eighth company, and will assure successively the position of the other guides.

Remarks.

278. A column by division at full distance will close to half distance by the same means and the same commands.

279. A column, by company, or by division, being at full or half distance, the colonel will cause it to close in mass by the same means and commands, substituting the indication, *column, close in mass,* for that of *to half distance, close column.* Each chief of subdivision will conform himself to all that has just been prescribed, except that he will not halt his subdivision till its guide shall be at a distance of six paces from the guide of the subdivision next preceding.

280. In a column, left in front, these various movements will be executed on the same principles.

Article Sixth.

To march in column at half distance, or closed in mass.

281. A column at half distance or in mass, being at a halt, the colonel will put it in march by the commands prescribed for a column at full distance.

282. The means of direction will also be the same for a column at half distance or in mass, as for a column at full distance, except that the general guides will not step out.

283. A column at half distance or in mass, being in march, when the colonel shall wish to

6 *   E

halt it, he will give the commands prescribed for halting a column at full distance, and if, afterwards, he judge it necessary to give a general direction to the guides of the column, he will employ, to this end, the commands and means indicated, No. 244 and following.

284. In columns at half distance or closed in mass, chiefs of subdivision will repeat the commands *march* and *halt,* as in columns at full distance.

285. The colonel will often march the column to the rear, by the means and the commands prescribed Nos. 170 and 171.

286. A column by division or company, whether at full or half distance or closed in mass, at a halt or marching, can be faced to the right or left, and marched off in the new direction.

Article Seventh.

To change direction in column at half distance.

287. A column at half distance, being in march, will change direction by the same commands and according to the same principles as a column at full distance; but as the distance between the subdivisions is less, the pivot man in each subdivision will take steps of fourteen inches instead of nine, and of seventeen inches instead of eleven, according to the gait, in order to clear, in time, the wheeling point, and the marching flank will describe the arc of a larger circle, the better to facilitate the movement.

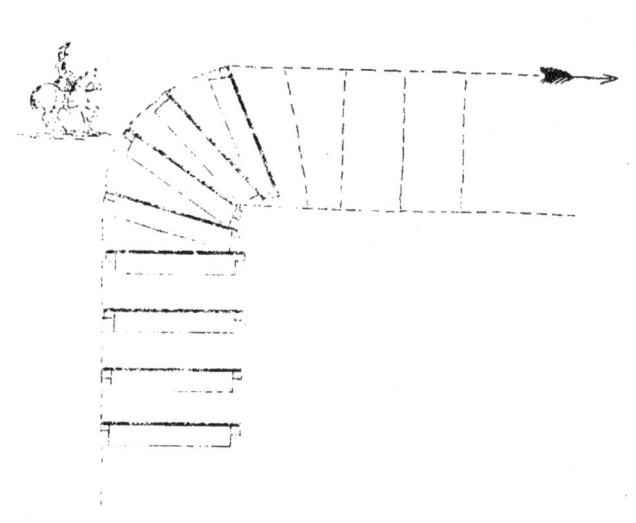
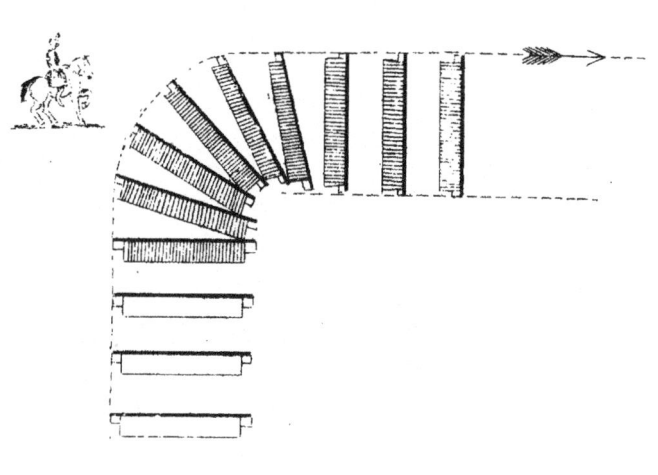

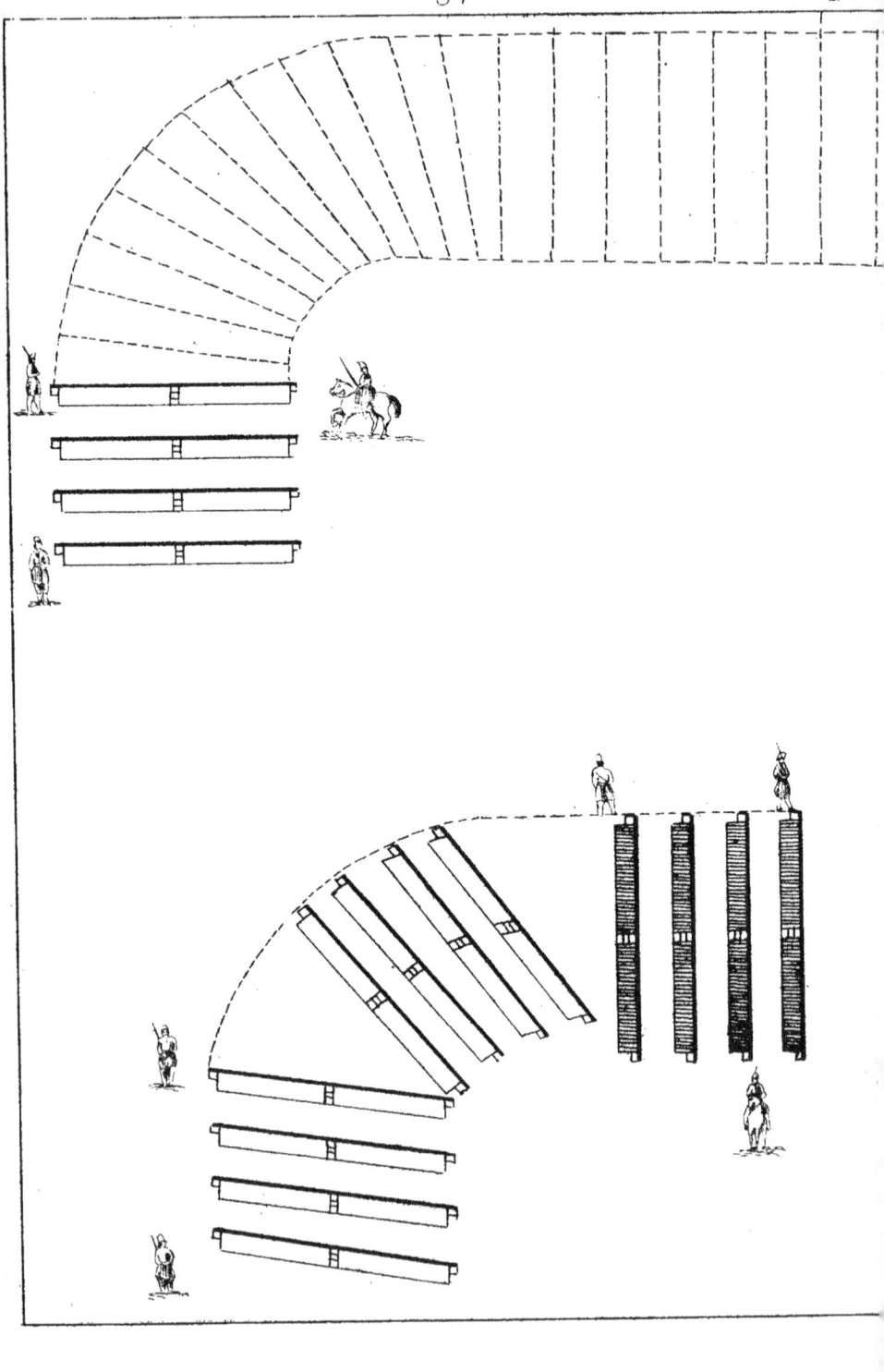

Article Eighth.

To change direction in column closed in mass.

1st. *To change direction in marching.*

288. A column by division, closed in mass, being in march, will change direction by the *front* of subdivisions.

289. Whether the change be made to the reverse, or to the pivot flank, it will always be executed on the principle of wheeling in marching; to this end, the colonel will first cause the battalion to take the guide on the flank opposite to the intended change of direction, if it be not already on that flank.

290. A column by division, closed in mass, right in front, having to change direction to the right, the colonel, after having caused a marker to be placed at the point where the change ought to commence, will command:

1. *Battalion, right wheel.* 2. March.

291. At the command *march*, the leading division will wheel as if it were part of a column at half distance.

292. The instant that this division commences the wheel, all the others will, at once, conform themselves to its movement; to this end the left guide of each, advancing slightly the left shoulder and lengthening a little the step, will incline to

the left, and will observe, at the same time, to gain so much ground to the front that there may constantly be an interval of four paces between his division and that which precedes it; and as soon as he shall cover the preceding guide, he will cease to incline and then march exactly in his trace.

293. Each division will conform itself to the movement of its guide; the men will feel lightly the elbow towards him and advance a little the left shoulder the instant the movement commences; each file, in inclining, will gain so much the less ground to the front, as the file shall be nearer to the pivot, and the right guide will gain only so much as may be necessary to maintain between his own and the preceding division the same distance which separates their marching flanks.

294. Each chief of division, turning to it, will regulate its march, and see that it remains constantly included between its guides, that its alignment continues nearly parallel to that of the preceding division, and that the centre bends only a little to the rear.

295. The colonel will superintend the movement, and cause the pivot of the leading division to lengthen or to shorten the step, conforming to he principle established, school of the company, o. 227 — if either be necessary to facilitate the ovement of the other divisions.

296. The lieutenant colonel, placed near the 't guide of the leading division, will regulate his .rch, and take care, above all, that he does not

throw himself *within* the arc he ought to describe.

298. The major, placed in the rear of the guides, will see that the last three conform themselves, each by slight degrees, to the movement of the guide immediately preceding, and that neither inclines too much in the endeavor to cover too promptly the guide in his front; he will rectify any serious fault that may be committed in either of those particulars.

298. The colonel, seeing the wheel nearly ended, will command:

1. *Forward.* 2. March.

299. At the second command, which will be given at the instant the leading division completes its wheel, it will resume the direct march; the other divisions will conform themselves to this movement; and if any guide find himself not covering his immediate leader, he will, by slight degrees, bring himself on the trace of that guide, by advancing the right shoulder.

300. If the column, right in front, has to change direction to the left, the colonel will first cause it to take the guide to the right, and then command:

1. *Battalion, left wheel.* 2. March.

301. At the command *march*, the battalion will change direction to the left, according to the principles just prescribed, and by inverse means.

302. When the battalion shall have resumed

the direct march, the colonel will change the guide to the left, on seeing the last three guides nearly in the direction of the one in front.

303. The foregoing changes of direction will be executed according to the same principles in a column, left in front.

304. A column by company, closed in mass, will change direction in marching, by the commands and means indicated for a column by division.

305. The guide who is the pivot of the particular wheel, ought to maintain himself at his usual distance of six paces from the guide who precedes him; if this distance be not exactly preserved, the divisions would necessarily become confounded, which must be carefully avoided.

2d. To change direction from a halt.

306. A column by company, or by division, closed in mass, being at a halt, when the colonel shall wish to give it a new direction, and in which it is to remain, he will cause it to execute this movement by the flanks of subdivisions, in the following manner:

307. The battalion having the right in front, when the colonel shall wish to cause it to change direction by the right flank, he will indicate to the lieutenant colonel the point of direction to the right; this officer will immediately establish, on the new direction, two markers, distant from each other a little less than the front of the first subdivision, the first marker in front of the right file of this subdivision; which being executed, he will command:

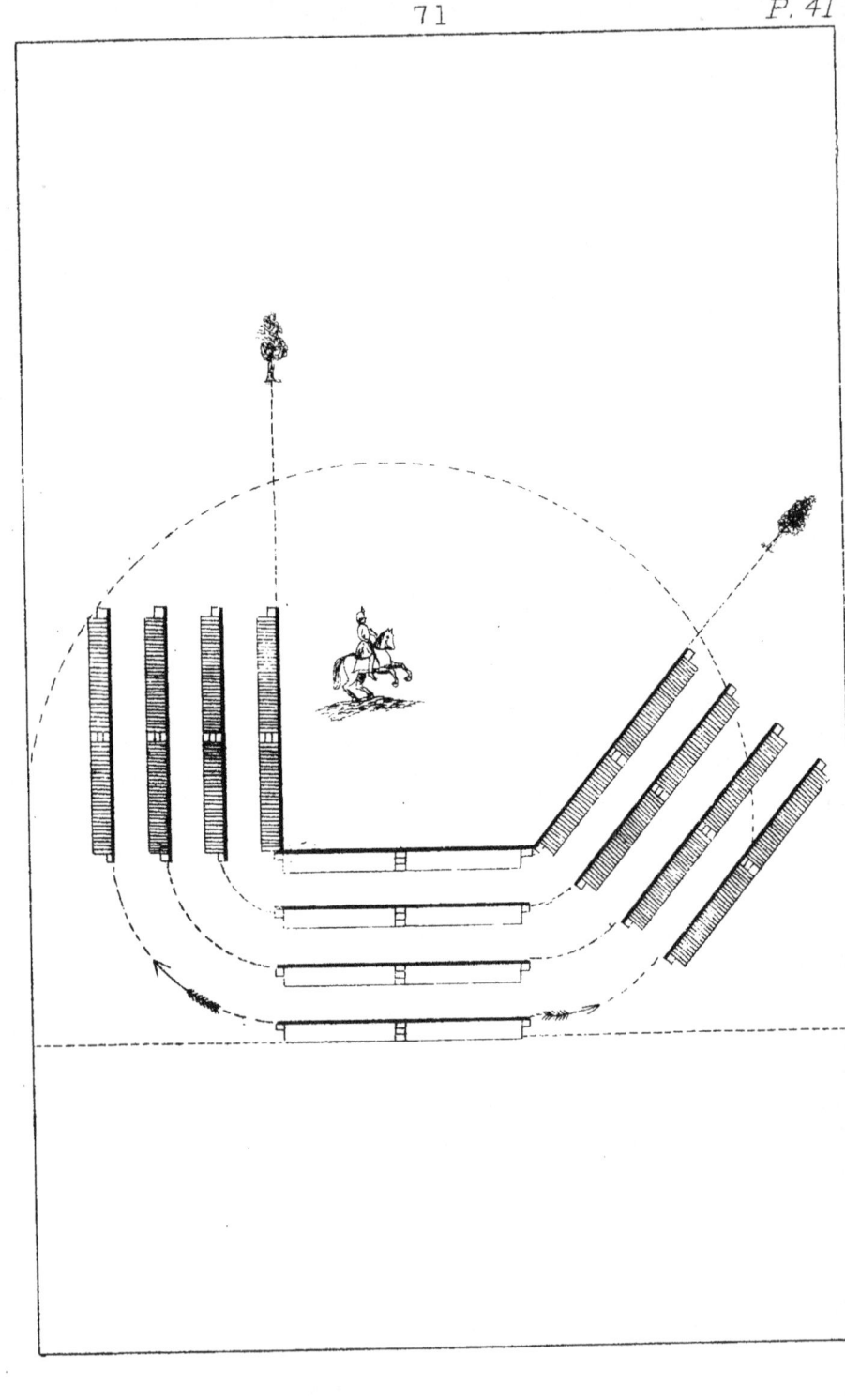

SCHOOL OF THE BATTALION—PART III. 71

1. *Change direction by the right flank.* 2. *Battalion, right*—FACE. 3. MARCH (or *double quick*—MARCH).

308. At the second command, the column will face to the right, and each chief of subdivision will place himself by the side of his right guide.

309. At the command *march*, all the subdivisions will step off together: the right guide of the leading one will direct himself from the first step, parallelly to the markers placed in advance on the new direction; the chief of the subdivision will not follow the movement, but see it file past, and as soon as the left guide shall have passed, he will command:

1. *First company* (or *first division*). 2. HALT. 3. FRONT. 4. *Left*—DRESS.

310. At the fourth command, the subdivision will place itself against the two markers, and be promptly aligned by its chief.

311. The right guide of each of the following subdivisions will conform himself to the direction of the right guide of the subdivision preceding his own in the column, so as to enter on the new direction parallelly to that subdivision, and at the distance of four paces from its rear rank.

312. Each chief of subdivision will halt in his own person, on arriving opposite to the left guides already placed on the new direction, see his subdivision file past, and conform himself, in halting and aligning it, to what is prescribed No. 309.

313. If the change of direction be by the left flank, the colonel will cause markers to be established as before, the first in front of the left file of the leading subdivision, and then give the same commands, substituting the indication *left* for *right*.

314. At the second command, all the subdivisions will face to the left, and each chief will place himself by the side of his left guide.

315. At the command *march*, all the subdivisions will step off together, each conducted by its chief.

316. The guide of the leading subdivision will direct himself, from the first step, parallelly to the markers; the subdivision will be conducted by its chief; and as soon as its left guide shall have passed the second marker, it will be halted and aligned as prescribed above; and so of each of the following subdivisions.

317. The colonel will hold himself on the designated flank, to see that each subdivision enters the new direction parallelly to the leading one, and at the prescribed distance from that which precedes.

318. The lieutenant colonel will place himself in front of, and facing to, the guide of the leading subdivision, and will assure the positions of the following guides, as they successively arrive on the new direction.

319. The major will follow the movement abreast with the last subdivision.

320. In order that this movement may be executed with facility and precision, it is necessary that the leading subdivision should entirely un-

mask the column; for example, the movement being made by the right flank, it is necessary, before halting the leading subdivision, that its left guide shall, at least, have arrived at the place previously occupied by its right guide, in order that each following subdivision which has to pass over a space at least equal to its front to put itself in the new direction, and whose left ought to pass the point at which the right had rested, may, at the command *halt*, find itself, in its whole front, parallel to the leading subdivision.

321. By this method there is no direction that may not be given to a column in mass.

Article Ninth.

Being in column at half distance, or closed in mass, to take distances.

322. A column at half distance will take full distances *by* the head of the column when it has to prolong itself on the line of battle. If, on the contrary, it has to form itself in line of battle on the ground it occupies, it will take distances *on* the leading or *on* the rearmost subdivision, according as the one or other may find itself at the point where the right or left of the battalion ought to rest in line of battle.

1*st.* *To take distances by the head of the column.*

323. The column being by company at half distance and at a halt, when the colonel shall wish to

cause it to take full distances by the head, he will command:

By the head of column, take wheeling distance.

324. At this command, the captain of the leading company will put it in march; to this end, he will command:

1. *First company, forward.* 2. *Guide left.*
3. March (or *double quick*—March).

325. When the second shall have nearly its wheeling distance, its captain will command:

1. *Second company, forward.* 2. *Guide left.*
3. March (or *double quick*—March).

326. At the command *march*, which will be pronounced at the instant that this company shall have its wheeling distance, it will step off smartly, taking the step from the preceding company. Each of the other companies will successively execute what has just been prescribed for the second.

327. The colonel will see that each company puts itself in march at the instant it has its distance.

328. The lieutenant colonel will hold himself at the head of the column, and direct the march of the leading guide.

329. The major will hold himself abreast with the rearmost guide.

330. If the column, instead of being at a halt,

SCHOOL OF THE BATTALION—PART III. 75

be in march, the colonel will give the same commands, and add:

MARCH (or *double quick*—MARCH).

331. If the column be marching in quick time, at the command *march*, the captain of the leading company will cause *double quick time* to be taken; which will also be done by the other captains as the companies successively attain their proper wheeling distance.

332. If the column be marching in *double quick time*, the leading company will continue to march at the same gait. The captains of the other companies will cause *quick time* to be taken, and as each company gains its proper distance, its captain will cause it to retake the *double quick step*.

2d. To take distances on the rear of the column.

333. If the colonel wish to take distances on the rearmost company, he will establish two markers on the direction he shall wish to give to the line of battle, the first opposite to the rearmost company, the second marker towards the head of the column, at company distance from the first, and both facing to the rear; at the same time, the right general guide, on an intimation from the lieutenant colonel, will move rapidly a little beyond the point to which the head of the column will extend, and place himself correctly on the prolongation of the two markers. These dispositions being made, the colonel will command:

1. *On the eighth company, take wheeling distance.*
2. *Column forward.* 3. *Guide left.* 4. MARCH
(or *double quick*—MARCH).

334. At the third command, the captains will place themselves two paces outside of the directing flank; the captain of the eighth company will caution it to stand fast.

335. At the command *march*, repeated by all the captains, except the captain of the eighth company, this latter company will stand fast; its chief will align it by the left on the first marker, who is opposite to this company, and place himself before its centre, after commanding: FRONT. At this command, the marker will retire, and the left guide will take his place.

336. All the other companies will put themselves in march, the guide of the leading one directing himself a little within the right general guide; when the seventh company has arrived opposite the second marker, its captain will halt, and align it on this marker, in the manner prescribed for the eighth company.

337. When the captain of the sixth company shall see that there is, between his company and the seventh, the necessary space for wheeling into line, he will halt his company; the guide facing to the rear will place himself promptly on the direction, and the moment he shall be assured in his position, the captain will align the company by the left, and then place himself two paces before its centre; the other companies will successively

SCHOOL OF THE BATTALION—PART III.

conform themselves to what has just been prescribed for the sixth company.

338. The colonel will follow the movement, and see that each company halts at the prescribed distance; he will promptly remedy any fault that may be committed, and, as soon as all the companies shall be aligned, he will cause the guides, who are faced to the rear, to face about.

339. The lieutenant colonel will successively assure the left guides on the direction, placing himself in their rear, as they arrive.

340. The major will hold himself at the head of the column, and will direct the march of the leading guide.

3d. To take distances on the head of the column.

341. The colonel, wishing to take distances on the leading company, will establish two markers in the manner just prescribed, one abreast with this company, and the other at company distance in rear of the first, but both facing to the front: the left general guide, on an intimation from the lieutenant colonel, will move rapidly to the rear and place himself correctly on the prolongation of the two markers, a little beyond the point to which the rear of the column will extend: these dispositions being made, the colonel will command:

1. *On the first company, take wheeling distance.*
2. *Battalion, about*—FACE. 3. *Column, forward.* 4. *Guide right.* 5. MARCH (or *double quick*—MARCH).

342. At the second command, all the companies, except the one designated, will face about, the guides remaining in the front rank, now become the rear.

343. At the fourth command, the captains will place themselves outside of their guides.

344. At the command *march*, the captain of the designated company will align it, as prescribed, No. 335, on the marker placed by its side.

345. The remaining companies will put themselves in march, the guide of the rearmost one will direct himself a little within the left general guide; when the second company shall have arrived opposite the second marker, its captain will face it about, conforming to what is prescribed, No. 270, and align it, as has just been prescribed for the first company.

346. The instant that the third company shall have its wheeling distance, its captain will halt it facing it about, as prescribed, No. 270, and align it by the left; the captains of the remaining companies will each, in succession, conform himself to what has just been prescribed for the captain of the third.

347. The colonel will follow the movement, as indicated No. 338; the lieutenant colonel and major will conform themselves to what is prescribed, Nos. 339 and 340.

348. These various movements will be executed according to the same principles in a column with the left in front.

349. They will be executed in like manner in a column closed in mass; but, if it be the wish of

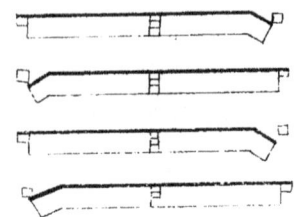

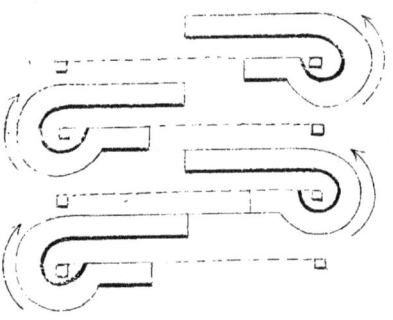

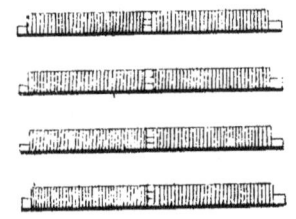

the colonel to open out the column to half, instead of full distance, he will substitute, in the commands, the indication *half*, for that of *wheeling distance*.

350. In a column by division, distances will be taken according to the same principles.

Article Tenth.

Countermarch of a column at full or half distance.

351. In a column at full or half distance, the countermarch will be executed by the means indicated, school of the company; to this end, the colonel will command:

1. *Countermarch.* 2. *Battalion right* (or *left*)— Face. 3. *By file left* (or *right*). 4. March (or *double quick*—March).

To countermarch a column closed in mass.

352. If the column be closed in mass, the countermarch will be executed by the commands and means subjoined.

353. The column being supposed formed by division, right in front, the colonel will command:

1. *Countermarch.* 2. *Battalion, right and left*— Face. 3. *By file left and right.* 4. March (or *double quick*—March).

354. At the first command, the chiefs of the odd numbered divisions will caution them to face to the right, and the chiefs of the others to face to the left.

355. At the second command, the odd divisions will face to the right, and the even to the left; the right and left guides of all the divisions will face about; the chiefs of odd divisions will hasten to their right and cause two files to break to the rear, and each chief place himself on the left of the leading front rank man of his division; the chiefs of even divisions will hasten to their left, and cause two files to break to the rear, and each chief place himself on the right of his leading front rank man.

356. At the command *march*, all the divisions, each conducted by its chief, will step off smartly, the guides standing fast; each odd division will wheel by file to the left around its right guide; each even division will wheel by file to the right around its left guide, each division so directing its march as to arrive behind its opposite guide, and when its head shall be up with this guide, the chief will halt the division, and cause it to face to the front.

357. Each division, on facing to the front, will be aligned by its chief by the right; to this end, the chiefs of the even divisions will move rapidly to the right of their respective divisions.

358. The divisions being aligned, each chief will command, FRONT; at this, the guides will shift to their proper flanks.

359. In a column with the left in front, the

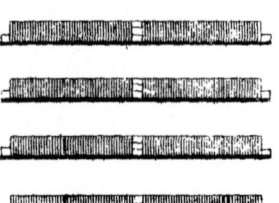

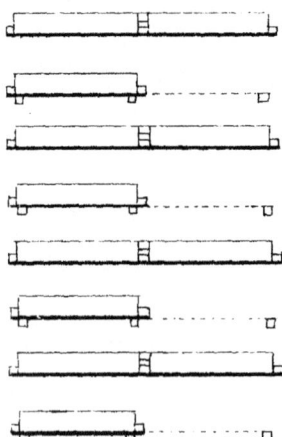

countermarch will be executed by the same commands and means; but all the divisions will be aligned by the left: to this end, the chiefs of the odd divisions will hasten to the left of their respective divisions as soon as the latter shall have been faced to the front.

360. The colonel, placed on the directing flank, will superintend the general movement.

361. The countermarch being ended, the lieutenant colonel will always place himself abreast with the leading, and the major abreast with the rearmost division.

362. In a column by company, closed in mass, the countermarch will be executed by the same means and commands, applying to companies what is prescribed for divisions.

363. The countermarch will always take place from a halt, whether the column be closed in mass, or at full, or half distance.

Article Eleventh.

Being in column by company, closed in mass, to form divisions.

364. The column being closed in mass, right in front, and at a halt, when the colonel shall wish to form divisions, he will command:

1. *Form divisions.* 2. *Left companies, left*—Face.
3. March (or *double quick*—March.)

365. At the first command, the captains of the left companies will caution them to face to the left.

366. At the second command, the left companies will face to the left, and their captains will place themselves by the side of their respective left guides.

367. The right companies, and their captains, will stand fast; but the right and left guides of each of these companies will place themselves respectively before the right and left files of the company, both guides facing to the right, and each resting his right arm gently against the breast of the front rank man of the file, in order to mark the direction.

368. At the command *march*, the left companies only will put themselves in march, their captains standing fast; as each shall see that his company, filing past, has nearly cleared the column, he will command:

1. *Such company.*   2. Halt.   3. Front.

369. The first command will be given when the company shall yet have four paces to march; the second at the instant it shall have cleared its right company; and the third immediately after the second.

370. The company having faced to the front, the files, if there be intervals between them, will promptly incline to the right; the captain will place himself on the left of the right company of the division, and align himself correctly on the front rank of that company.

SCHOOL OF THE BATTALION—PART III. 83

371. The left guide will place himself at the same time before one of the three left files of his company, face to the right, and cover correctly the guides of the right company; the moment his captain sees him established on the direction, he will command:

Right—DRESS.

372. At this, the left company will dress forward on the alignment of the right company; the front rank man, who may find himself opposite to the left guide, will, without preceding his rank, rest lightly his breast against the right arm of this guide; the captain of the left company will direct its alignment on this man, and the alignment being assured, he will command, FRONT; but not quit his position.

373. The colonel seeing the divisions formed, will command:

Guides—POSTS.

374. At this, the guides who have marked the fronts of divisions will return to their places in column, the left guide of each right company passing through the interval in the centre of the division, and the captains will place themselves as prescribed No. 75.

375. The colonel, from the directing flank of the column, will superintend the general execution of the movement.

376. If the column be in march, instead of at a

halt, when the colonel shall wish to form divisions, he will command:

1. *Form divisions.* 2. *Left companies, by the left flank.* 3. March (or *double quick*—March).

377. At the first command, the captains of the right companies will command, *Mark time*, the captains of the left companies will caution their companies to *face by the left flank.*

378. At the third command, the right companies will mark time, the left companies will face to the left; the captains of the left companies will each see his company file past him, and when it has cleared the column, will command:

Such company by the right flank—March.

As soon as the divisions are formed, the colonel will command:

4. *Forward.* 5. March.

379. At the fifth command, the column will resume the gait at which it was marching previous to the commencement of the movement. The guides of each division will remain on the right and left of their respective companies; the left guide of the right company will pass into the line of file closers, before the two companies are united; the right guide of the left company will step into the rear rank. The captains will place themselves as prescribed No. 75.

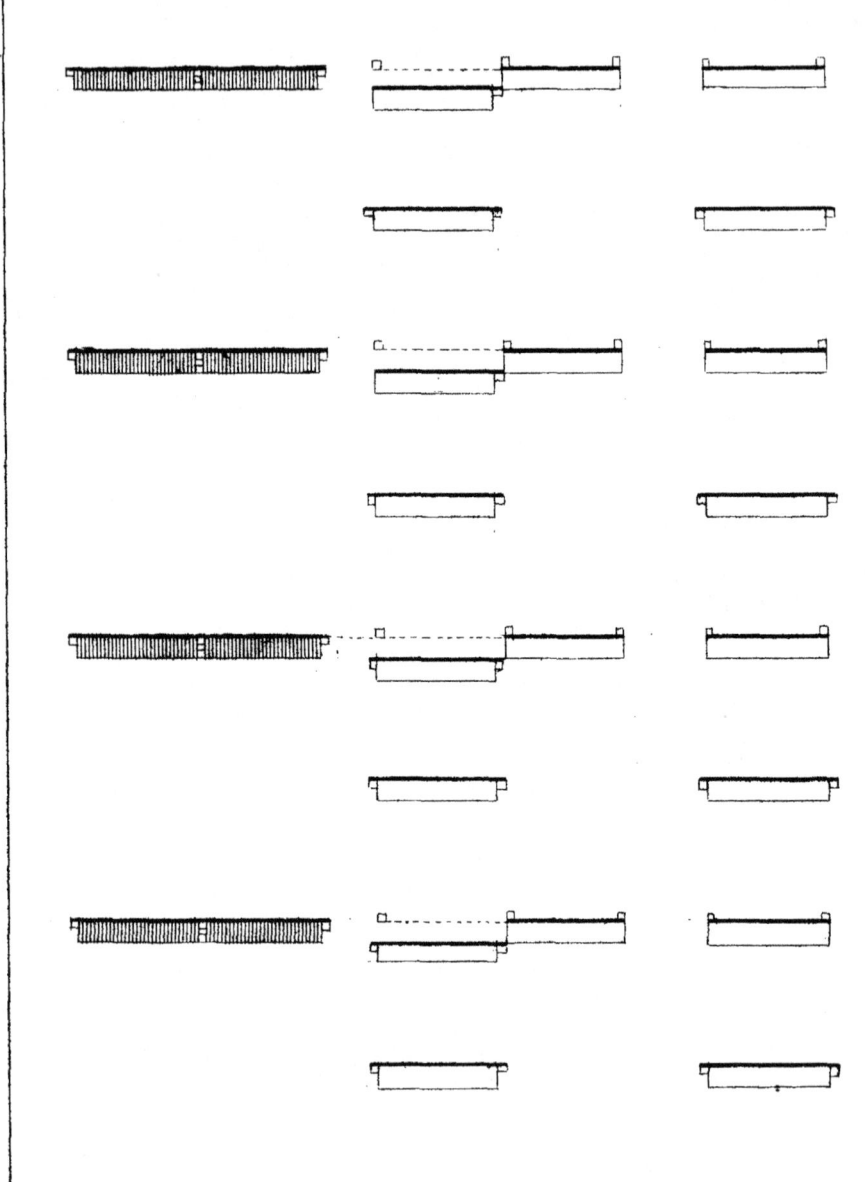

SCHOOL OF THE BATTALION—PART III.

Being in column at full or half distance to form divisions.

380. If the column be at a halt, and, instead of being closed in mass, is at full or half distance, divisions will be formed in the same manner; but the captains of the left companies, if the movement be made in quick time, after commanding FRONT, will each place himself before the centre of his company, and command, 1. *Such company, forward.* 2. *Guide right.* 3. MARCH. If the movement be made in double quick time, each will command as soon as his company has cleared the column:

1. *Such company by the right flank.* 2. MARCH.

381. The right guide of each left company will so direct his march as to arrive by the side of the man on the left of the right company. The left company being nearly up with the rear rank of the right company, its captain will halt it, and the movement will be finished as prescribed No. 371 and following.

382. If the left be in front, the movement will be executed by inverse means: the right companies will conform themselves to what is prescribed above for the left companies; and the two guides, placed respectively, before the right and left files of each left company, will face to the left. At the command, *Guides posts,* given by the colonel, the guides, who have marked the front of divisions, and the captains, will quickly retake their places in the column.

383. If the column be marching at full distance, the divisions will be formed as prescribed No. 196 If it be marching at half distance, the formation

VOL. II.—8

will take place by the commands and according to the principles indicated No. 376 ; if the column be marching in double quick time, the companies which should mark time will march in quick time by the command of their captains.

Remarks on the formation of divisions from a halt.

384. As this movement may be considered as the element of deployments, it ought to be executed with the utmost accuracy.

385. If companies marching by the flank do not preserve exactly their distances, there will be openings between the files at the instant of facing to the front.

386. If captains halt their companies too early, they will want space, and the files which have not cleared the flanks of the standing companies will not be able to dress into line without pushing their ranks laterally.

387. If on the contrary the companies be halted too late, it will be necessary for them to incline to the right or left in dressing; and in deployments, either of these faults would lead to error in the following companies.

388. As often as a guide shall have to step out to place himself before his subdivision in order to mark the direction, he will be particularly careful to place himself so as to be opposite to one of the three outer files of the subdivision when they shall be aligned : if he take too much distance, and neither of those files finds itself against him, the chiefs of the subdivision will have no assured point on which to direct the alignment.

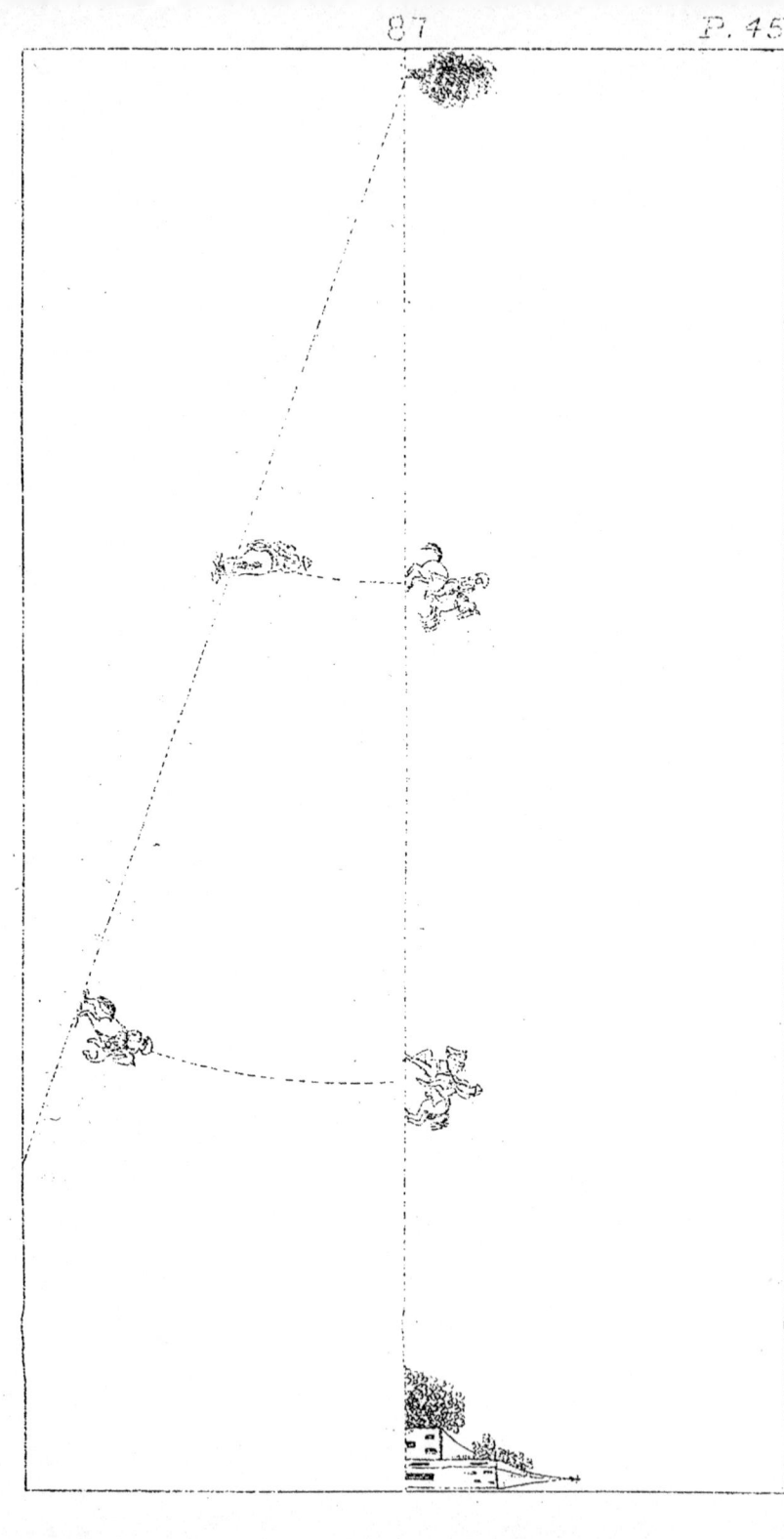

PART FOURTH.

Different modes of passing from the order in column to the order in battle.

ARTICLE FIRST.

Manner of determining the line of battle.

389. The line of battle may be marked or determined in three different manners: 1*st*, by placing two markers eighty or a hundred paces apart, on the direction it is wished to give to the line; 2*d*, by placing a marker at the point at which it may be intended to rest a flank, and then choosing a second point towards, or beyond the opposite flank, and there posting a second marker distant from each other a little less than the leading subdivision; 3*d*, by choosing at first the points of direction for the flanks, and then determining, by intermediate points, the straight line between those selected points, both of which may sometimes be beyond reach.

ARTICLE SECOND.

Different modes of passing from column at full distance into line of battle.

1. To the left (or right)
2. On the right (or left)
3. Forward,
4. Faced to the rear,

} into line of battle.

1st. *Column at full distance, right in front, to the left into line of battle.*

390. A column, right in front, being at a halt, when the colonel shall wish to form it to the left into line, he will assure the positions of the guides by the means previously indicated, and then command:

1. *Left into line, wheel.* 2. MARCH (or *double quick*—MARCH).

391. At the first command, the right guide of the leading company will hasten to place himself on the direction of the left guides of the column, face to them, and place himself so as to be opposite to one of the three right files of his company, when they shall be in line: he will be assured in this position by the lieutenant colonel.

392. At the command *march*, briskly repeated by the captains, the left front rank man of each company will face to the left, and rest his breast lightly against the right arm of his guide; the companies will wheel to the left on the principle of wheeling from a halt, conforming themselves to what is prescribed, school of the company, No. 239: each captain will turn to his company, to observe the execution of the movement, and, when the right of the company shall arrive at three paces from the line of battle, he will command:

1. *Such company.* 2. HALT.

393. The company being halted, the captain will place himself on the line by the side of the left front rank man of the company next on the right, align himself correctly, and command:

3. *Right*—Dress.

394. At this command, the company will dress up between the captain and the front rank man on its left, the captain directing the alignment on that man; the front rank man on the right of the right company, who finds himself opposite to its right guide, will lightly rest his breast against the left arm of this guide.

395. Each captain, having aligned his company, will command, Front, and the colonel will add:

Guides—Posts.

396. At this command, the guides will return to their places in line of battle, each passing through the nearest captain's interval; to permit him to pass, the captain will momentarily step before the first file of his company, and the covering sergeant behind the same file. *This rule is general for all the formations into line of battle.*

397. When companies form line of battle, file closers will always place themselves exactly two paces from the rear rank, which will sufficiently assure their alignment.

398. The battalion being correctly aligned, the colonel, lieutenant colonel, and major, as well as the adjutant and sergeant major, will return to their respective places in line of battle. *This rule*

is general for all the formations into line of battle; nevertheless, the battalion being in the school of elementary instruction, the colonel will go to any point he may deem necessary.

399. A column, with the left in front, will form itself *to the right into line of battle*, according to the same principles; the left guide of the left company will place himself, at the first command, on the direction of the right guides, in a manner corresponding to what is prescribed, No. 391, for the right guide of the right company.

400. At the command *guides posts*, the captains will take their places in line of battle as well as the guides. *This rule is general for all formations into line of battle in which the companies are aligned by the left.*

401. A column by division may form itself into line of battle by the same commands, and means, but observing what follows: if the right be in front, at the command *halt*, given by the chiefs of division, the left guide of each right company will place himself on the alignment opposite to one of the three files on the left of his company; the left guide of the first company will be assured on the direction by the lieutenant colonel; the left guides of the other right companies will align themselves correctly on the division guides; to this end, the division guides (on the alignment) will invert, and hold their pieces up perpendicularly before the centre of their bodies, at the command *left into line, wheel.* If the column by division be with the left in front, the right guides of left companies will conform themselves to what has just been prescribed for the left guides of right companies, and

place themselves on the line opposite to one of the three right files of their respective companies.

402. A column in march will be formed into line, without halting, by the same commands and means. At the command *march*, the guides will halt in their places, and the lieutenant colonel will promptly rectify their positions.

403. If, in forming the column into line, the colonel should wish to move forward, without halting, he will command:

1. *By companies left wheel.* 2. MARCH (or *double quick*—MARCH).

404. At the command *march*, briskly repeated by the captains, each company will wheel to the left on a fixed pivot, as prescribed in the school of the company, No. 261; the left guides will step back into the rank of file closers before the wheel is completed, and when the right of the companies shall arrive near the line, the colonel will command:

3. *Forward.* 4. MARCH. 5. *Guide centre.*

405. At the fourth command, given at the instant the wheel is completed, the companies will march directly to the front. At the fifth command, the color and the general guides will move rapidly six paces to the front. The colonel will assure the direction of the color; the captains of companies and the men will, at once, conform themselves to the principles of the march in line of battle, to be hereinafter indicated, No. 587, and following.

406. The same principles are applicable to a column left in front.

By inversion to the right (or *left*) *into line of battle.*

407. When a column, right in front, shall be under the necessity of forming itself into line faced to the reverse flank, and the colonel shall wish to execute this formation by the shortest movement, he will command:

1. *By inversion, right into line, wheel.* 2. *Battalion, guide right.*

408. At the first command, the lieutenant-colonel will place himself in front, and facing to the right guide of the leading subdivision; at the second command, he will rectify, as promptly as possible, the direction of the right guides of the column; the captain of the odd company, if there be one, and the column be by division, will promptly bring the right of his company on the direction, and at company distance from the division next in front; the left guide of the leading subdivision will place himself on the direction of the right guides, and will be assured in his position by the lieutenant colonel; which being executed, the colonel will command:

3. MARCH (or *double quick*—MARCH).

409. At this, the right front rank man of each subdivision will face to the right, rest his breast lightly against the left arm of his guide, and the

battalion will form itself to the right into line of battle, according to the principles prescribed; which being executed, the colonel will command:

Guides—Posts.

410. If the column be with the left in front, it will form itself, by inversion, to the left into line, according to the same principles.

411. If the colonel should wish the battalion, when formed into line of battle, to be moved forward, the movement will be executed by the commands, and according to the principles indicated in No. 403; always preceding the command, *by companies right* (or *left*) *wheel*, by the command, *by inversion.*

Successive Formations.

412. Under the denomination of successive formations are included all those formations where the several subdivisions of a column arrive one after another on the line of battle; such are formations on the right, or left, forward and faced to the rear into line of battle, as well as deployments of columns in mass.

413. The successive formations which may be ordered when the column is marching, and is to continue marching, will be executed by a combination of the two gaits, *quick* and *double quick* time.

2d. *Column at full distance, on the right* (or *on the left*), *into line of battle.*

414. A column by company, at full distance and right in front, having to form itself on the right into line of battle, the colonel will indicate to the lieutenant colonel a little in advance, the point of *appui*, or rest, for the right, as well as the point of direction to the left; the lieutenant colonel will hasten with two markers, and establish them in the following manner on the direction indicated.

415. The first marker will be placed at the point of *appui* for the right front rank man of the leading company; the second will indicate the point where one of the three left files of the same company will rest when in line; they will be placed so as to present the right shoulder to the battalion when formed.

416. These dispositions being made, the colonel will command:

1. *On the right, into line.* 2. *Battalion, guide right.*

417. At the second command, the right will become the directing flank, and the touch of the elbow will be to that side; the right guide of the leading company will march straight forward until up with the turning point, and each following guide will march in the trace of the one immediately preceding.

418. The leading company being nearly up with the first marker, its captain will command: 1. *Right turn*, and when the company is precisely up with this marker, he will add: 2. March.

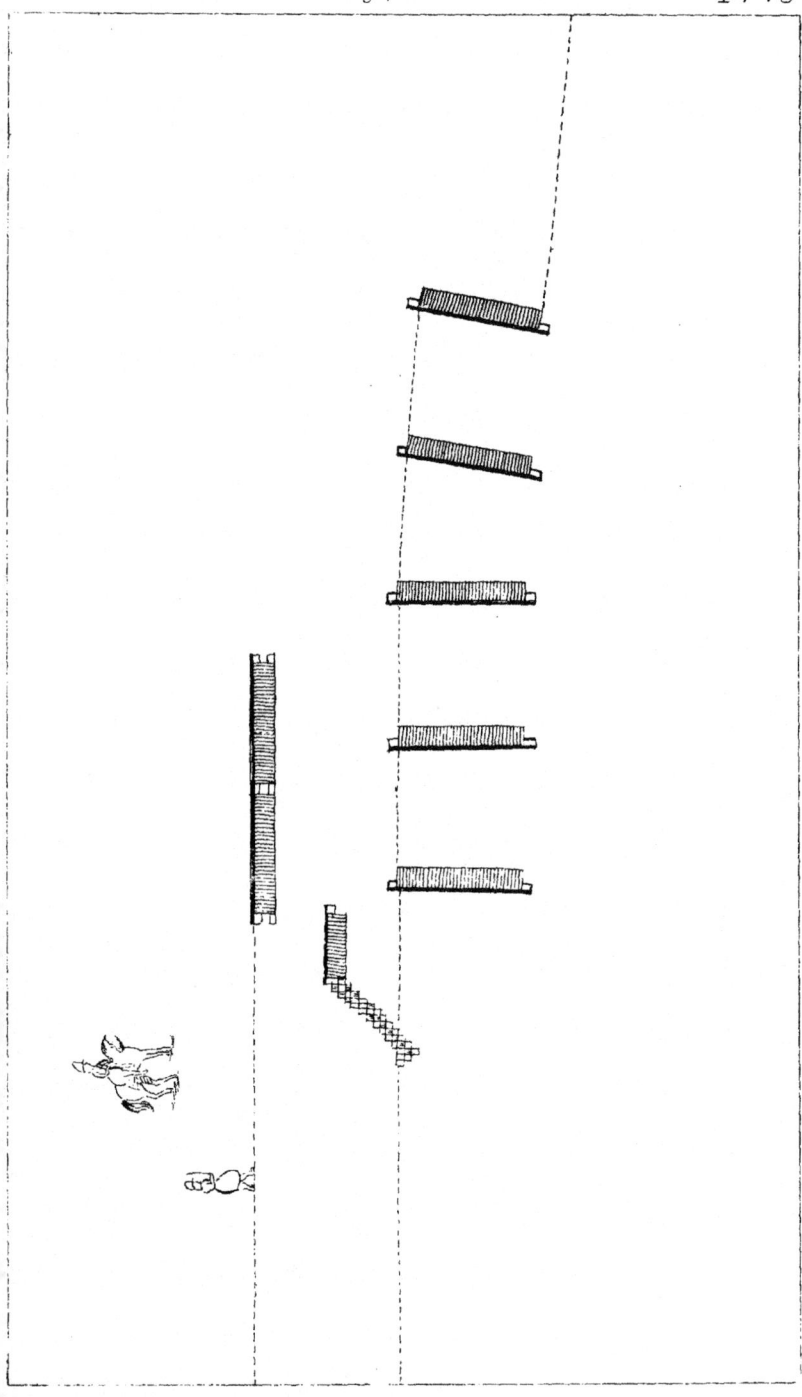

P. 46.

419. At the command *march*, the company will turn to the right; the right guide will so direct himself as to bring the man next to him opposite to the right marker, and when at three paces from him, the captain will command:

1. *First company;* 2. Halt.

420. At the second command, the company will halt; the files, not yet in line, will form promptly; the left guide will retire as a file closer; and the captain will then command:

3. *Right*—Dress.

421. At this command, the company will align itself; the two men who find themselves opposite to the two markers, will each lightly rest his breast against the right arm of his marker; the captain, passing to the right of the front rank, will direct the alignment on these two men. *These rules are general for all successive formations.*

422. The second company will continue to march straight forward; when arrived opposite to the left flank of the preceding company, it will turn to the right, and be formed on the line of battle, as has just been prescribed; the right guide will direct himself so as to come upon that line by the side of the man on the left of the first company.

423. At the distance of three paces from the line of battle, the company will be halted by its captain, who will place himself briskly by the side

of the man on the left of the preceding company, and align himself correctly on its front rank.

424. The left guide will, at the same time, place himself before one of the three left files of his company, and, facing to the right, he will place himself accurately on the direction of the two markers of the preceding company.

425. The captain will then command:

Right—DRESS.

426. At this command, the second company will dress forward on the line; the captain will direct its alignment on the front rank man who has rested his breast against the left guide of the company.

427. The following companies will thus come successively to form themselves on the line of battle, each conforming itself to what has just been prescribed for the one next to the right; and when they shall all be established, the colonel will command:

Guides—POSTS.

428. At this command, the guides will take their places in line of battle, and the markers placed before the right company will retire.

429. If the column be marching in quick time, and the colonel should wish to cause the movement to be executed in double quick time, he will add the command: *Double quick*—MARCH. At the command *march*, all the companies will take the double quick step, and the movement

will be executed as prescribed, No. 417, and following.

430. The colonel will follow up the formation, passing along the front, and being always opposite to the company about to turn: it is thus that he will be the better able to see and to correct the error that would result from a command given too soon or too late to the preceding company.

431. The lieutenant colonel will, with the greatest care, assure the direction of the guides; to this end, the instant that the markers are established for the leading company, he will move a little beyond the point at which the left of the next company will rest, establish himself correctly on the prolongation of the two markers, and assure the guide of the second company on this direction; this guide being assured, the lieutenant colonel will place himself farther to the rear, in order to assure, in like manner, the guide of the third company, and so on, successively, to the left of the battalion. In assuring the guides in their positions on the line of battle, he will take care to let them first place themselves, and confine himself to rectifying their positions if they do not cover accurately, and at the proper distance, the preceding guides or markers. *This rule is general, for all successive formations.*

432. A column, left in front, will form itself on the left into line of battle according to the same principles: the captains will go to the left of their respective companies to align them, and shift afterwards to their proper flanks, as prescribed No. 400.

Remarks on the formation on the right, or left, *into* line of battle.

433. In order that this movement may be executed with regularity, it is necessary to establish the line of battle so that the guide of each company, after turning, may have at least ten steps to take, in order to come upon that line.

434. In the first exercises, the line of battle will be established on a direction parallel to that of the column: but, when the captains and guides shall comprehend the mechanism of the movement, the colonel will generally choose oblique directions, in order to habituate the battalion to form itself in any direction.

435. When the direction of the line of battle forms a sensible angle with that of the march of the column, the colonel, before beginning the movement, will give the head of the column a new direction parallel to that line: to this end, he will indicate to the guide of the leading company a point in advance, on which this guide will immediately direct himself, and the company will conform itself to the direction of its guide, at the command, or on a mere caution, of the captain, according as the change of direction may require; each following company will make the same movement, on the same ground, as it shall successively arrive. By this means the guides of all the companies in the column will have, after turning, nearly the same number of paces to take in order to come upon the line of battle.

436. Every captain will always observe, in

placing himself on that line, not to give the command *dress*, until after the guide of his company shall have been assured on the direction by the lieutenant colonel. *This rule is general for all successive formations.*

437. Each captain will cause his company to support arms, the instant that the captain, who follows him, shall have commanded *front*. *This rule is general for all successive formations.*

438. When, in the execution of this movement, the colonel shall wish to commence firing, he will give the order to that effect to the captain whose company is the first in line of battle; this captain will immediately place himself behind the centre of his company, and as soon as the next captain shall have commanded *front*, he will commence the fire by file, by the commands prescribed, school of the company. At the command *fire by file*, the marker at the outer file of this first company will retire, and the other will place himself against the nearest man of the next company. The captain of the latter will commence firing as soon as the captain of the third company, in line, shall have commanded *front;* the marker before the nearest file of the second company, in line, will now retire, and the guide before the opposite flank will place himself before the nearest file of the third company, in line, and so on, in continuation, to the last company on the left or right of the battalion, according as the formation may have commenced with the right or left in front.

439. In all the successive formations, the same principles will be observed for the execution of the fire by file. This fire will always be executed by the command of each captain of company.

3d. Column at full distance, forward into line of battle.

440. A column being by company, at full distance, right in front, and at a halt, when the colonel shall wish to form it forward into line, he will conform to what is prescribed Nos. 414 and 415, and then command:

1. *Forward into line.* 2. *By company, left half wheel.* 3. MARCH (or *double quick*—MARCH).

441. At the first command, the captain of the leading company will add — *guide right*, put the company in march, halt it three paces from the markers, and align it against the latter by the right.

442. At the command *march*, all the other companies will wheel to the left on fixed pivots; and, at the instant the colonel shall judge, according to the direction of the line of battle, that the companies have sufficiently wheeled, he will command:

4. *Forward.* 5. MARCH. 6. *Guide right.*

443. At the fifth command, the companies, ceasing to wheel, will march straight forward; and at the sixth, the men will touch elbows towards the right. The right guide of the second company, who is nearest to the line of battle, will march straight forward; each succeeding right guide will follow the file immediately before him at the cessation of the wheel.

444. The second company having arrived oppo-

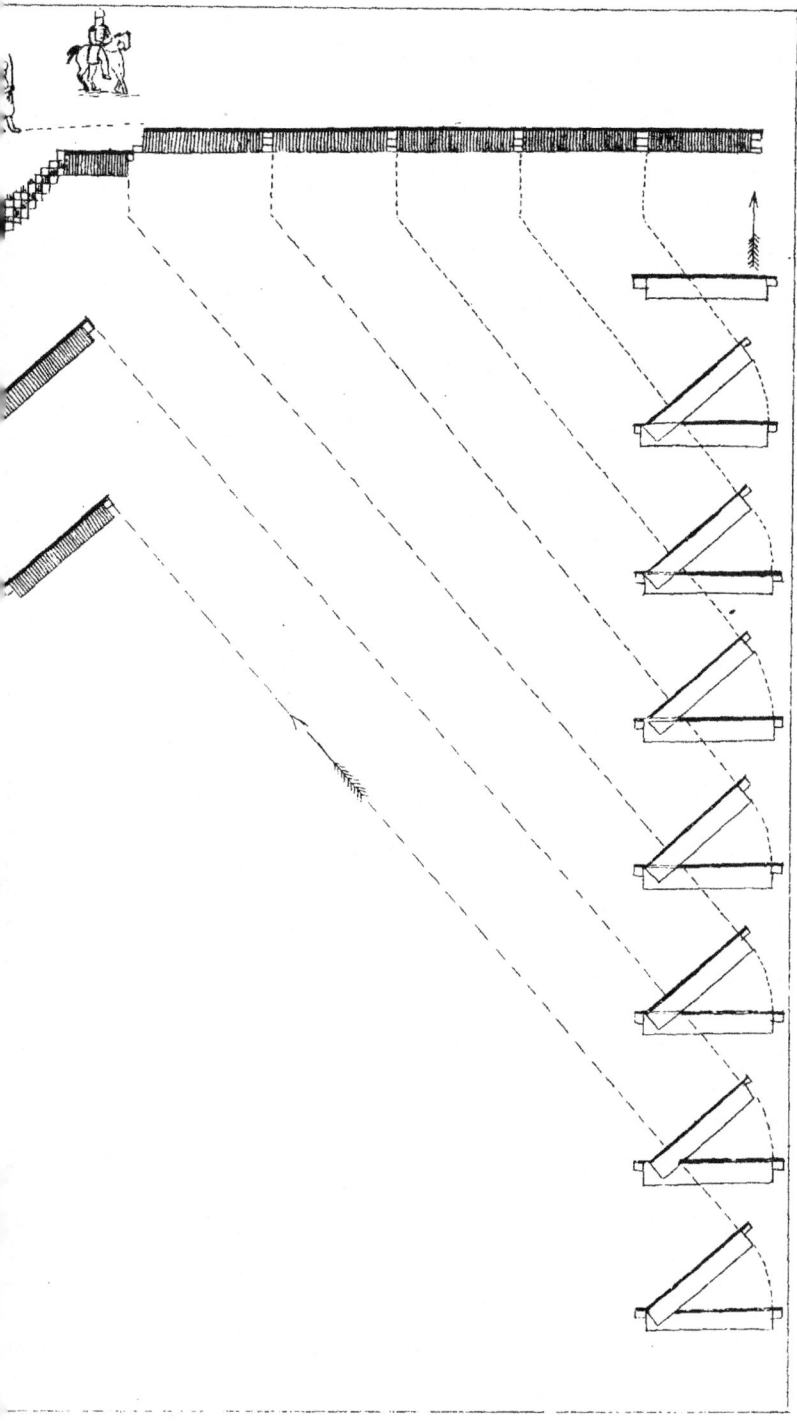

SCHOOL OF THE BATTALION—PART IV. 101

site to the left file of the first, its captain will cause it to turn to the right, in order to approach the line of battle; and when its right guide shall be at three paces from that line, the captain will command:

1. *Second company.* 2. HALT.

445. At the second command, the company will halt; the files not yet in line with the guide will come into it promptly, the left guide will place himself on the line of battle, so as to be opposite to one of the three files on the left of the company; and, as soon as he is assured on the direction by the lieutenant colonel, the captain, having placed himself accurately on the line of battle, will command:

3. *Right*—DRESS.

446. At the instant that the guide of the second company begins to turn to the right, the guide of the third, ceasing to follow the file immediately before him, will march straight forward; and, when he shall arrive opposite to the left of the second, his captain will cause the company to turn to the right, in order to approach the line of battle, halt it at three paces from that line, and align it by the right, as prescribed for the second company.

447. Each following company will execute what has just been prescribed for the third, as the preceding company shall turn to the right, in order to approach the line of battle.

448. The formation ended, the colonel will command:

Guides—Posts.

449. The colonel and lieutenant colonel will observe in this formation, what is prescribed for them on the right into line.

450. A column left in front, will form itself forward into line of battle according to the same principles and by inverse means.

451. When a column by company at full distance, right in front, and in march, shall arrive behind the right of the line on which it is to form into battle, the colonel and lieutenant colonel will conform themselves to what is prescribed Nos. 414 and 415.

452. The head of the column having arrived at company distance from the two markers established on the line, the colonel will command:

1. *Forward into line.* 2. *By company, left half wheel.* 3. March (or *double quick*—March).

453. At the first command, the captain of the first company will command, *Guide right*, and caution it to march directly to the front, the captains of the other companies will caution them to wheel to the left.

454. At the command *march*, briskly repeated by the captains, the first company will continue to march to the front, taking the touch of elbows to the right. Its chief will halt it at three paces from the markers, and align it by the right. The other companies will wheel to the left on fixed

pivots, and at the instant the colonel shall judge that they have wheeled sufficiently, he will command:

4. *Forward.* 5. MARCH. 6. *Guide right.*

455. At the fifth command, the companies will cease to wheel and move forward. At the sixth, they will take the touch of elbows to the right. The movement will be executed as previously explained.

456. If the colonel should wish to form the column forward into line, and to continue to march in this order, he will not cause markers to be established; the movement will be executed in *double quick time*, by the same commands and means, but with the following modifications.

457. At the first command, the captain of the first company will add *quick time* after the command *guide right.* At the second command, the first company will continue to march in quick time, and will take the touch of elbows to the right; its chief will immediately place himself on its right, and to assure the march, will take points of direction to the front. The captain of the second company will cause his company to take the same gait as soon as it shall arrive on a line with the first, and will also move to the right of his company; the captains of the third and fourth companies will execute successively what has just been prescribed for the second. The companies will preserve the touch of elbows to the right, until the command, *guide centre.*

458. When the color company shall have

entered the line, the colonel will command, *guide centre.* At this command, the color-bearer and the right general guide will move rapidly six paces in advance of the line. The colonel will assure the direction of the color-bearer. The lieutenant colonel and the right companies will immediately conform themselves to the principles of the march in line of battle. The left companies and the left general guide, as they arrive on the line, will also conform to the same principles. If the column be marching in double quick time, when the last company shall have arrived on the line, the colonel will cause the double quick to be resumed.

459. It is not necessary that the movement be entirely completed, before halting the battalion. As soon as the part of the battalion already formed shall have arrived on the line of battle, the colonel will halt the battalion; the companies not in line will each complete the movement.

Remarks on the formation forward, into line of battle.

460. The precision of this movement depends on the direction the companies have at the moment the colonel commands, *Forward*—MARCH. The colonel will judge nicely the point of time for giving this command, observing that, if the direction of the line of battle form with that of the column a right, or nearly a right angle, the companies ought to wheel about the eighth of the circle, and that the more acute the angle formed by the two directions, so much the more the compa-

nies ought to wheel before marching straight forward.

461. It is important that each company in marching towards the line of battle should turn exactly opposite the point where its captain ought to place himself on that line; if a company turn too soon, it will find itself masked, in part, by that which preceded it on the line of battle, and be obliged to unmask itself by the oblique step; if it turn too late, it will leave an interval between itself and the preceding company to be regained in like manner. In either case, the next company will be led into error, and the fault propagated to the opposite flank of the battalion.

462. The guide of each company ought so to regulate himself in turning, as to bring his company to the halting point parallelly with the line of battle.

463. If the angle formed by the line of battle and the primitive direction of the column be so acute, that the companies, on arriving opposite to their respective places on the line of battle, find themselves nearly parallel to it, the captains will not give the command, *right* (or *left*) *turn*, but each halt his company, place himself on the line, and command:

Right (or *left*)—DRESS.

464. If, on the contrary, the angle formed by the line of battle and the primitive direction of the column be much greater than a right angle, the formation should be executed, not by the movement *forward into line of battle*, but by that of *on the*

right (or *left*) *into line of battle*, and according to the principles prescribed for this formation.

465. If a company encounter an obstacle sufficient to prevent it from marching by the front, it will *right* (or *left*) *face* in marching, by the commands and means indicated in the school of the company, Nos. 314 and 315. The guide will continue to follow the same file behind which he was marching, and will maintain exactly the same distance from the company immediately preceding his own. The obstacle being passed, the company will be formed into line by the command of its captain.

4th. Column at full distance, faced to the rear, into line of battle.

466. A column being by company, at full distance, right in front, and at a halt, when the colonel shall wish to form it into line faced to the rear, he and the lieutenant colonel will conform themselves to what is prescribed Nos. 414 and 415, and the colonel will then command:

1. *Into line, faced to the rear.* 2. *Battalion, right* —Face. 3. March (or *double quick*—March).

467. At the first command, the captain of the leading company will cause it to face to the right, and put it in march, causing it to wheel by file to the left, and direct its march towards the line of battle which it will pass in rear of the left marker; the first file having passed three paces beyond the line, the company will wheel again by

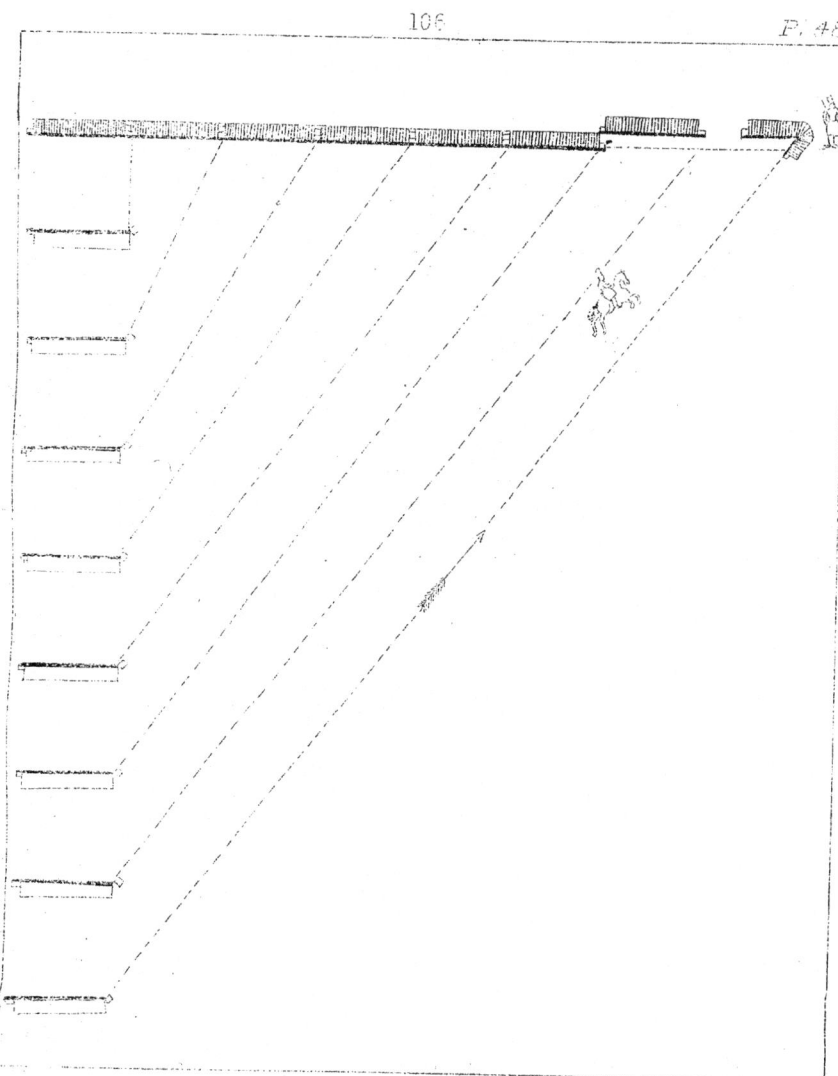

file to the left, in order to place itself in rear of the two markers; being in this position, its captain will halt it, face it to the front, and align it by the right against the markers.

468. At the second command, all the other companies will face to the right, each captain placing himself by the side of his right guide.

469. At the command *march*, the companies will put themselves in movement; the left guide of the second, who is nearest to the line of battle, will hasten in advance to mark that line; he will place himself on it as prescribed above for successive formations, and thus indicate to his captain the point at which he ought to pass the line of battle, by three paces, in order to wheel by file to the left, and then to direct his company parallelly to that line.

470. As soon as the first file of this company shall have arrived near the left file of the preceding one already on the line of battle, its captain will command:

1. *Second company.* 2. Halt. 3. Front. 4. *Right*—Dress.

471. The first command will be given when the company shall yet have four paces to take to reach the halting point.

472. At the second command, the company will halt.

473. At the third, the company will face to the front, and if there be openings between the files, the latter will promptly close to the right; the captain will immediately place himself by the side

of the man on the left of the preceding company, and align himself on its front rank.

474. The fourth command will be executed as prescribed, No. 426.

475. The following companies will be conducted and established on the line of battle as just prescribed for the second, each regulating itself by the one that precedes it; the left guides will detach themselves in time to precede their respective companies on the line by twelve or fifteen paces, and each place himself so as to be opposite to one of the three left files of his company, when in line. If the movement be executed in double quick time, the moment it is commenced, all the left guides will detach themselves at the same time from the column, and will move at a run, to establish themselves on the line of battle.

476. The formation ended, the colonel will command:

Guides—Posts.

477. The colonel and lieutenant colonel, in this formation, will each observe what is prescribed for him in that of *on the right, into line of battle*.

478. A column, left in front, will form itself faced to the rear into line of battle according to the same principles and by inverse means.

479. If the column be in march, and should arrive in front of the right of the line on which it is to form into battle, the colonel and lieutenant colonel will conform to what is prescribed, Nos. 414 and 415.

480. When the head of the column shall be

nearly at company distance from the two markers established on the line, the colonel will command:

1. *Into line, faced to the rear.* 2. *Battalion, by the right flank.* 3. MARCH (or *double quick—*MARCH).

481. At the first command, the captains will caution their companies to face by the right flank.

482. At the command *march*, briskly repeated by the captains of companies, all the companies will face to the right; the first company will then wheel by file to the left, and be directed by its captain a little to the rear of the left marker; then pass three paces beyond the line, and wheel again by file to the left; having arrived on the line, the captain will halt the company, and align it by the right. The remaining part of the movement will be executed as heretofore explained.

483. The foregoing principles are applicable to a column, left in front.

484. As the companies approach the line of battle, it is necessary that their captains should so direct the march as to cross that line a little in rear of their respective guides, who are faced to the basis of the formation; hence each guide ought to detach himself in time to find himself correctly established on the direction before his company shall come up with him.

Article Third.

Formation in line of battle by two movements.

485. If a column by company, right in front, and at a halt, find itself in part on the line of battle, and the colonel should think proper to form line of battle before all the companies enter the new direction, the formation will be executed in the following manner:

486. It will be supposed that the column has arrived behind the line of battle, and that five companies have entered the new direction. The colonel having assured the guides of the first five companies on the direction, will command:

1. *Left into line, wheel.*   2. *Three rear companies, forward into line.*

487. At the second command, the chief of each of the rear companies will command: *By company, left half wheel;* and the colonel will add:

3. March (or *double quick*—March).

488. At this command, briskly repeated, the first five companies will form themselves *to the left, into line of battle*, and the three last *forward, into line of battle*, by the means prescribed for these respective formations; each captain of the three rear companies will, when his company shall have sufficiently wheeled, command:

1. *Forward.* 2. March. 3. *Guide right.*

489. If the column be in march, the colonel will command:

1. *To the left, and forward into line.* 2. March (or *double quick*—March).

490. At the first command, the captains of those companies which have not entered on the new direction, will command: *By company, left half wheel.* At the command *march*, briskly repeated, the first five companies will form left into line, and the last three forward into line, as prescribed for these respective formations. Those captains who form their companies forward into line will conform to what is prescribed, No. 488.

491. If the colonel should wish, in forming the battalion into line, to march it immediately forward, he will command:

1. *By company to the left, and forward into line.* 2. March.

492. At the first command, each captain, whose company is not yet in the new direction, will command: 1. *By company, left half wheel;* 2. *Double quick.* At the command *march*, briskly repeated by the captains, the companies not in the new direction will execute what is prescribed above for forming forward into line while marching; each of the other companies will wheel to the left on a fixed pivot, and when the right of these

companies shall arrive on the line, the colonel will command:

    3. *Forward.*   4. March.   5. *Guide centre.*

493. The fifth command will be given when the color-bearer arrives on the line, if not already there.

494. If the battalion be marching in double quick time, the colonel will cause quick time to be taken before commencing the movement.

495. If, instead of arriving behind, the column should arrive before the line of battle, the colonel will command:

1. *Left into line, wheel.* 2. *Three rear companies into line, faced to the rear.*

496. At the second command, the captain of each of the three rear companies will command: 1. *Such company*; 2. *Right*—Face. The colonel will then add:

    3. March (or *double quick*—March).

497. At this command, briskly repeated, the first five companies will form themselves *to the left, into line of battle,* and the three last *faced to the rear, into line of battle,* by the means prescribed for these respective formations.

498. If the column be in march, the colonel will command:

1. To the left, and into line faced to the rear.
2. March (or *double quick*—March).

499. The movement will be executed as prescribed Nos. 391, 480, and following.
500. These several movements in a column, left in front, will be executed according to the same principles, and by inverse means.

Article Fourth.

Different modes of passing from column at half distance, into line of battle.

1. To the left (or right)
2. On the right (or left)
3. Forward, by deployment,
4. Faced to the rear,
} into line of battle.

1st. *Column at half distance, to the left (or right) into line of battle.*

501. A column at half distance having to form itself to the left (or right) into line of battle, the colonel will cause it to take distances by one of the means prescribed, Article IX., Part Third, of this school; which being executed, he will form the column into line of battle, as has been indicated, No. 390, and following.
502. If a column by company, at half distance, be in march, and it be necessary to form rapidly into line of battle, the colonel will command:

1. *By the rear of column left* (or *right*) *into line, wheel.* 2. March (or *double quick*—March).

503. At the first command, the right general guide will move rapidly to the front, and place himself a little beyond the point where the head of the column will rest, and on the prolongation of the guides. The captain of the eighth company will command: *Left into line, wheel;* the other captains will caution their companies to continue to march to the front.

504. At the command *march*, briskly repeated by the captain of the eighth company, the guide of this company will halt short, and the company will wheel to the left, conforming to the principles prescribed for wheeling from a halt; when its right shall arrive near the line, the captain will halt the company, and align it by the left. The other captains will place themselves briskly on the flank of the column; when the captain of the seventh sees there is sufficient distance between his company and the eighth to form the latter into line, he will command: *Left into line, wheel*—March; the left guide will halt short, and facing to the rear, will place himself on the line; the company will wheel to the left, the man on the left of the front rank will face to the left, and place his breast against the left arm of the guide; the captain will halt the company when its right shall arrive near the line, and will align it by the left. The other companies will conform successively to what has just been prescribed for the seventh.

505. Each captain will direct the alignment of his company on the left man in the front rank of the company next on his right.

506. The lieutenant colonel will be watchful that the leading guide marches accurately on the prolongation of the line of battle, and directs himself on the right general guide. The major, placed in rear of the left guide of the eighth company, will, as soon as the guide of the seventh company is established on the direction, hasten in rear of the guides of the other companies, so as to assure each of them in succession on the line.

2d. Column at half distance, on the right (or left) into line of battle.

507. A column at half distance will form itself on the right (or left) into line of battle, as prescribed for a column at full distance.

3d. Column at half distance, forward, into line of battle.

508. If it be wished to form a column at half distance, forward into line of battle, the colonel will first cause it to close in mass and then deploy it on the leading company.

4th. Column at half distance, faced to the rear, into line of battle.

509. A column at half distance will be formed into line of battle, faced to the rear, as prescribed for a column at full distance.

Article Fifth.

Deployment of columns closed in mass.

510. A column in mass may be formed into line of battle:

1. Faced to the front, by the deployment.
2. Faced to the rear, by the countermarch and the deployment.
3. Faced to the right and faced to the left, by a change of direction by the flank, and the deployment.

511. When a column in mass, by division, arrives behind the line on which it is intended to deploy it, the colonel will indicate, in advance, to the lieutenant colonel, the direction of the line of battle, as well as the point on which he may wish to direct the column. The lieutenant colonel will immediately detach himself with two markers, and establish them on that line, the first at the point indicated, the second a little less than the front of a division from the first.

512. Deployments will always be made upon lines parallel, and lines perpendicular to the line of battle; consequently, if the head of the column be near the line of battle, the colonel will commence by establishing the direction of the column perpendicularly to that line, if it be not already so, by one of the means indicated, No. 244 and following, or No. 307 and following. If the co-

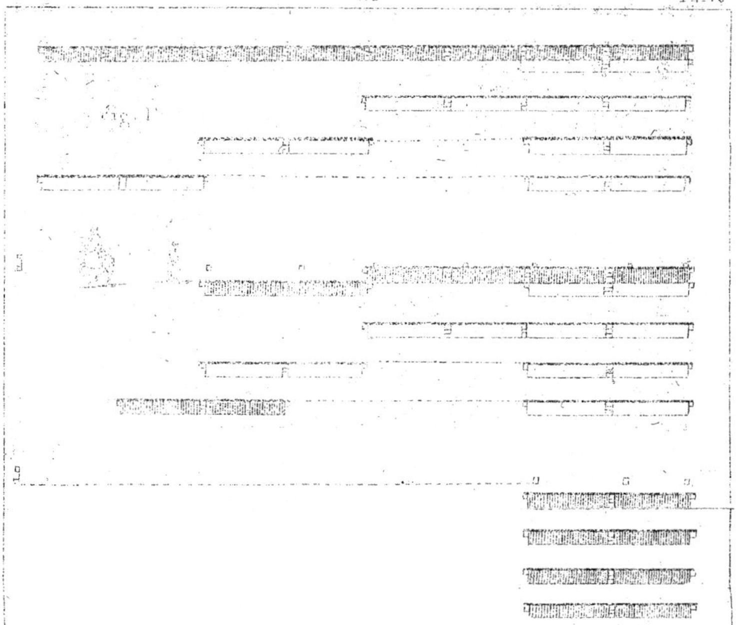

Pl. 43

Fig. 1.

Fig. 2.

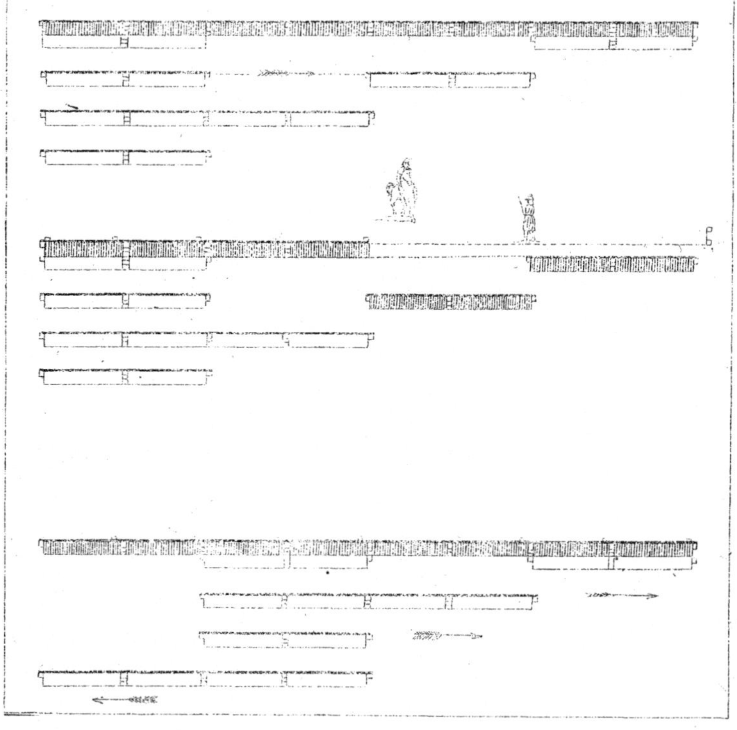

SCHOOL OF THE BATTALION—PART IV. 117

lumn be in march, he will so direct it that it may arrive exactly behind the markers, perpendicularly to the line of battle, and halt it at three paces from that line.

513. The column, right in front, being halted, it is supposed that the colonel wishes to deploy it on the first division; he will order the left general guide to go to a point on the line of battle a little beyond that at which the left of the battalion will rest when deployed, and place himself correctly on the prolongation of the markers established before the first division.

514. These dispositions being made, the colonel will command:

1. *On the first division, deploy column.* 2. *Battalion, left*—FACE.

515. At the first command, the chief of the first division will caution it to stand fast; the chiefs of the three other divisions will remind them that they will have to face to the left.

516. At the second command, the three last divisions will face to the left; the chief of each division will place himself by the side of its left guide, and the junior captain by the side of the covering sergeant of the left company, who will have stepped into the front rank.

517. At the same command, the lieutenant colonel will place a third marker on the alignment of the two first, opposite to one of the three left files of the right company, first division, and then place himself on the line of battle a few paces

beyond the point at which the left of the second division will rest.

518. The colonel will then command:

3. March (or *double quick*—March).

519. At this command, the chief of the first division will go to its right, and command:

Right—Dress.

520. At this, the division will dress up against the markers; the chief of the division, and its junior captain, will each align the company on his left, and then command:

Front.

521. The three divisions, faced to the left, will put themselves in march; the left guide of the second will direct himself parallelly to the line of battle; the left guides of the third and fourth divisions will march abreast with the guide of the second; the guides of the third and fourth, each preserving the prescribed distance between himself and the guide of the division which preceded his own in the column.

522. The chief of the second division will not follow its movement; he will see it file by him, and when its right guide shall be abreast with him, he will command:

1. *Second division.* 2. Halt. 3. Front.

523. The first command will be given when the division shall yet have seven or eight paces to march; the second, when the right guide shall be abreast with the chief of the division, and the third immediately after the second.

524. At the second command, the division will halt; at the third, it will face to the front, and if there be openings between the files, the chief of the division will cause them to be promptly closed to the right; the left guides of both companies will step upon the line of battle, face to the right, and place themselves on the direction of the markers established before the first division, each guide opposite to one of the three left files of his company.

525. The division having faced to the front, its chief will place himself accurately on the line of battle, on the left of the first division; and when he shall see the guides assured on the direction, he will command, *Right*—DRESS. At this, the division will be aligned by the right in the manner indicated for the first.

526. The third and fourth divisions will continue to march; at the command *halt*, given to the second, the chief of the third will halt in his own person, place himself exactly opposite to the guide of the second, after this division shall have faced to the front and closed its files; he will see his division file past, and when his right guide shall be abreast with him, he will command:

1. *Third division.* 2. HALT. 3. FRONT.

527. As soon as the division faces to the front,

its chief will place himself two paces before its centre, and command:

1. *Third division, forward.* 2. *Guide right.*
3. March.

528. At the third command, the division will march towards the line of battle; the right guide will so direct himself as to arrive by the side of the man on the left of the second division, and when the division is at three paces from the line of battle, its chief will halt it and align it by the right.

529. The chief of the fourth division will conform himself (and the chief of the fifth, if there be a fifth) to what has just been prescribed for the third.

530. The deployment ended, the colonel will command:

Guides—Posts.

531. At this command, the guides will resume their places in line of battle, and the markers will retire.

532. If the column be in march, and the colonel shall wish to deploy it on the first division without halting the column, he will make the dispositions indicated Nos. 512 and 513, and when the first division shall have arrived at three paces from the line, he will command:

1. *On the first division, deploy column.* 2. *Battalion by the left flank.* 3. March (or *double quick*—March).

SCHOOL OF THE BATTALION—PART IV. 121

533. At the first command, the chief of the first division will caution it to halt, and will command, *First division;* the other chiefs will caution their divisions to face by the left flank.

534. At the command *march,* briskly repeated by the chiefs of the rear divisions, the chief of the first division will command, HALT, and will align his division by the right against the markers; the other divisions will face to the left, their chiefs hastening to the left of their divisions. The second division will conform its movements to what is prescribed Nos. 522 and following. The third and fourth divisions will execute what is prescribed Nos. 526 and following; but the chief of each division will halt in his own person at the command march given by the chief of the division which precedes him, and when the right of his division arrives abreast of him, he will command:

Such division, by the right flank—MARCH.

535. The lieutenant colonel will assure the position of the guides, conforming to what is prescribed No. 431. The major will follow the movement abreast with the fourth division.

536. If the colonel shall wish to deploy the column without halting it, and to continue the march, the markers will not be posted; the movement will be executed by the same commands and the same means as the foregoing, but with the following modifications:

537. At the first command, the chief of the first division will command, 1 *Guide right.* 2. *Quick time.* At the command, *Double quick*—MARCH,

VOL. II.—11

given by the colonel, the first division will march in quick time and will take the touch of elbows to the right; the captains will place themselves on the right of their respective companies; the captain on the right of the battalion will take points on the ground to assure the direction of the march. The chief of the second division will allow his division to file past him, and when he sees its right abreast of him, he will command, 1. *Second division by the right flank.* 2. March. 3. *Guide right*, and when this division shall arrive on the alignment of the first, he will cause it to march in quick time. The third and fourth divisions will deploy according to the same principles as the second.

538. The colonel, lieutenant colonel, major, and color-bearer will conform themselves to what is prescribed No. 458.

539. The colonel will see, pending the movement, that the principles just prescribed are duly observed, and particularly that the divisions, in deploying, be not halted too soon nor too late. He will correct promptly and quickly the faults that may be committed, and prevent their propagation. *This rule is general for all deployments.*

540. The column being at a halt, if, instead of deploying it on the first, the colonel shall wish to deploy it on the rearmost division, he will cause the dispositions to be made indicated No. 511 and following; but it will be the right general guide whom he will send to place himself beyond the point at which the right of the battalion will rest when deployed.

541. The colonel will then command:

SCHOOL OF THE BATTALION—PART IV. 123

1. *On the fourth* (or such) *division, deploy column.*
2. *Battalion, right*—FACE.

542. At the first command, the chief of the fourth division will caution it to stand fast; the chiefs of the other divisions will caution them that they will have to face to the right.

543. At the second command, the first three divisions will face to the right; and the chief of each will place himself by the side of its right guide.

544. At the same command, the lieutenant colonel will place a third marker between the first two, so that this marker may be opposite to one of the three right files of the left company of the division; the lieutenant colonel will then place himself on the line of battle a few paces beyond the point at which the right of the third division will rest when deployed.

545. The colonel will then command:

3. MARCH (or *double quick*—MARCH).

546. At this command, the three right divisions will put themselves in march, the guide of the first so directing himself as to pass three paces within the line marked by the right general guide. The chief of the third division will not follow its movement; he will see it file past, halt it when its left guide shall be abreast with him, and cause it to face to the front; and, if there be openings between the files, he will cause them to be promptly closed to the left.

547. The chief of the fourth division, when he sees it nearly unmasked by the three others, will command:

1. *Fourth division, forward.* 2. *Guide left.* 3. **March.**

548. At the command *march*, which will be given the instant the fourth is unmasked, this division will approach the line of battle, and when at three paces from the markers on that line, its chief will halt it, and command:

Left—**Dress.**

549. At this command, the division will dress forward against the markers; the chief of the division and the junior captain will each align the company on his right, and then command:

Front.

550. The instant that the third division is unmasked, its chief will cause it to approach the line of battle, and halt it in the manner just prescribed for the fourth.

551. The moment the division halts, its right guide and the covering sergeant of its left company will step on the line of battle, placing themselves on the prolongation of the markers established in front of the fourth division; as soon as they shall be assured in their positions, the division will be aligned as has just been prescribed for the fourth.

552. The second and first divisions which will have continued to march, will, in succession, be halted and aligned by the left, in the same manner as the third; the chiefs of these divisions will conform themselves to what is prescribed, No. 526. The second being near the line of battle, the command will not be given for it to move on this line but it will be dressed up to it.

553. The deployment ended, the colonel will command:

Guides—Posts.

554. At this command, the chiefs of division and the guides will resume their places in line of battle, and the markers will retire.

555. The lieutenant colonel will assure the positions of the guides by the means indicated, No. 431, and the major will follow the movement abreast with the fourth division.

556. If the column be in march, and the colonel shall wish to deploy it on the fourth division, he will make the dispositions indicated, No. 511 and following; and when the head of the column shall arrive within three paces of the line, he will command:

1. *On the fourth division, deploy column.* 2. *Battalion, by the right flank.* 3. March (or *double quick*—March).

557. At the first command, the chief of the fourth division will caution it to halt, and will command, *Fourth division:* the chiefs of the

other divisions will caution their divisions to *face to the right.*

558. At the command *march*, briskly repeated by the chiefs of the first three divisions, the chief of the fourth will command: Halt. The first three divisions will face to the right, and be directed parallelly to the line of battle. The chief of each of these divisions will place himself by the side of its right guide. The chief of the third division will see his division file past him, and when his left guide is abreast of him, he will halt it, and face it to the front. The chief of the fourth division, when he shall see it nearly unmasked, will command: 1. *Fourth division, forward;* 2. *Guide left;* 3. March (or *double quick*—March). This division will move towards the line of battle, and when at three paces from this line, it will be halted by its chief, and aligned by the left.

559. The chief of the third division will move his division forward, conforming to what has just been prescribed for the fourth.

560. The chiefs of the second and first divisions, after halting their divisions, will conform to what is prescribed, No. 552.

561. If the colonel should wish to deploy on the fourth division without halting the column, and to continue to march forward, he will not have markers posted, and the movement will be executed by the same commands and the same means, with the following modifications: the fourth division, when unmasked, will be moved forward in quick time, and will continue to march, instead of being halted, and will take the touch of elbows to the left. The third division, on being unmasked,

will be moved to the front in double quick time, but when it arrives on the alignment of the fourth it will take the quick step, and dress to the left until the command *Guide centre*, is given by the colonel. The chiefs of the second and first divisions will conform to what has been prescribed for the third. When the first division shall arrive on the line, the colonel may cause the battalion to take the double quick step.

562. The colonel and lieutenant colonel will conform to what has been prescribed, Nos. 458 and 459.

563. To deploy the column on an interior division, the colonel will cause the line to be traced by the means above indicated, and the general guides will move briskly on the line, as prescribed, Nos. 513 and 540. This being executed, the colonel will command:

1. *On such division, deploy column.* 2. *Battalion outwards—*FACE. 3. MARCH (or *double quick—*MARCH).

564. Whether the column be with the right or left in front, the divisions which, in the order in battle, belong to the right of the directing one, will face to the right; the others, except the directing division, will face to the left; the divisions in front of the latter will deploy by the means indicated, No. 542, and following; those in its rear will deploy as is prescribed, No. 513, and following.

565. The directing division, the instant it finds itself unmasked, will approach the line of battle.

taking the guide left or right, according as the right or left of the column may be in front. The chief of this division will align it by the directing flank, and then step back into the rear, in order momentarily to give place to the chief of the next for aligning the next division.

566. The lieutenant colonel will assure the positions of the guides of divisions, which, in the line of battle, take the right of the directing division, and the major will assure the positions of the other guides.

567. If the column be in march, the colonel will command:

1. *On such division, deploy column.* 2. *Battalion, by the right and left flanks.* 3. March (or *double quick*—March).

568. The divisions which are in front of the directing one will deploy by the means indicated, Nos. 557, and following; those in rear, as prescribed, No. 533, and following.

569. The directing division, when unmasked, will conform to what is prescribed for the fourth division, No. 558.

570. The colonel, lieutenant colonel and major will conform to what has been prescribed, Nos. 458 and 459.

571. In a column, left in front, deployments will be executed according to the same principles, and by inverse means.

Remarks on the deployment of columns, closed in mass.

572. All the divisions ought to deploy rectangularly, to march off abreast, and to preserve their distances towards the line of battle.

573. Each division, the instant that it is unmasked, ought to be marched towards the line of battle, and to be aligned upon it by the flank next to the directing division; the latter, whether the right or left be in front, will always be aligned by the flank next to the point of *appui*, when the deployment is made on the first or last division; but if the column be deployed on an interior division, this division will be aligned by the flank which *was* that of direction.

574. The chiefs of division will see that, in deploying, the principles prescribed for marching by the flank are well observed, and if openings between the files occur, which ought not to happen except on broken or difficult grounds, the openings ought to be promptly closed towards the directing flank as soon as the divisions face to the front.

575. If a chief of division give the command *halt*, or the command, *by the right or left flank*, too soon or too late, his division will be obliged to oblique to the right or left in approaching the line of battle, and his fault may lead the following subdivision into error.

576. In the divisions which deploy by the left flank, it is always the left guide of each company who ought to place himself on the line of battle, to

mark the direction; in divisions which deploy by the right flank, it is the right guide.

577. A column by company, closed in mass, may be formed to the left or to the right into line, in the same manner as a column at half distance, and by the means indicated, No. 502, and following.

578. A column by company, closed in mass, may be formed on the right or on the left into line of battle, as a column at half distance; but in order to execute this movement, withont arresting the march of the column, it is necessary that the guides avoid, with the greatest care, shortening the step in turning, and that the men near them, respectively, conform themselves rapidly to the movements of their guides.

Remarks on inversions.

579. Inversions giving frequently the means of forming line of battle, in the promptest manner, are of great utility in the movements of an army.

580. The application that may be made of inversions in the formations to the right and to the left in line of battle, has been indicated, No. 407, and following. They may also be advantageously employed in the successive formations, except in that of *faced to the rear, into line of battle.*

581. Formations, by inversion, will be executed according to the same principles as formations in the direct order; but the colonel's first command will always begin *by inversion.*

582. The battalion being in line of battle by in-

version, when the colonel shall wish, by forming it into column, to bring it back to the direct order, he will cause it either to *break* or to *ploy* by company, or by division, accordingly as the column may have been by company or by division before it had been formed into line of battle by inversion.

583. When a battalion in line of battle, formed by inversion, has to be ployed into column, the movement will be executed according to the same principles as if the line were in the direct order, but observing what follows.

584. If it be intended that the column shall be by division, with the first in front, or by company, with the first company in front, the colonel will announce in the second command—*left in front*, because the battalion being in line of battle by inversion, that subdivision is on the left.

585. Each chief whose subdivision takes position in the column in front of the directing one, will conduct his subdivision till it halts; and each chief whose subdivision takes position in rear of the directing one, will halt in his own person when up with the preceding right guide, and see his subdivision file past; and each chief will align his subdivision by the right. When the column is to be put in march, the second command will be—*guide left*, because the proper right is in front.

586. For the same reason, if it be intended that the last subdivision shall be in front, *right in front*, will be announced in the second command; the subdivisions will be aligned by the left, and

to put the column in march, the second command will be, *guide right,* because the proper left is in front.

PART FIFTH.

Article First.

To advance in line of battle.

587. The battalion being correctly aligned, and supposed to be the directing one, when the colonel shall wish to march in line of battle, he will give the lieutenant colonel an intimation of his purpose, place himself about forty paces in rear of the color-file, and face to the front.

588. The lieutenant colonel will place himself a like distance in front of the same file, and face to the colonel, who will establish him as correctly as possible, by signal of the sword, perpendicularly to the line of battle opposite to the color-bearer. The colonel will next, above the heads of the lieutenant colonel and color-bearer, take a point of direction in the field beyond, if a distinct one present i'self, exactly in the prolongation of those first two points.

589. The colonel will then move twenty paces farther to the rear, and establish two markers on the prolongation of the straight line passing through the color-bearer and the lieutenant colonel; these markers will face to the rear, the first placed about twenty-five paces behind the rear

133 P. 50

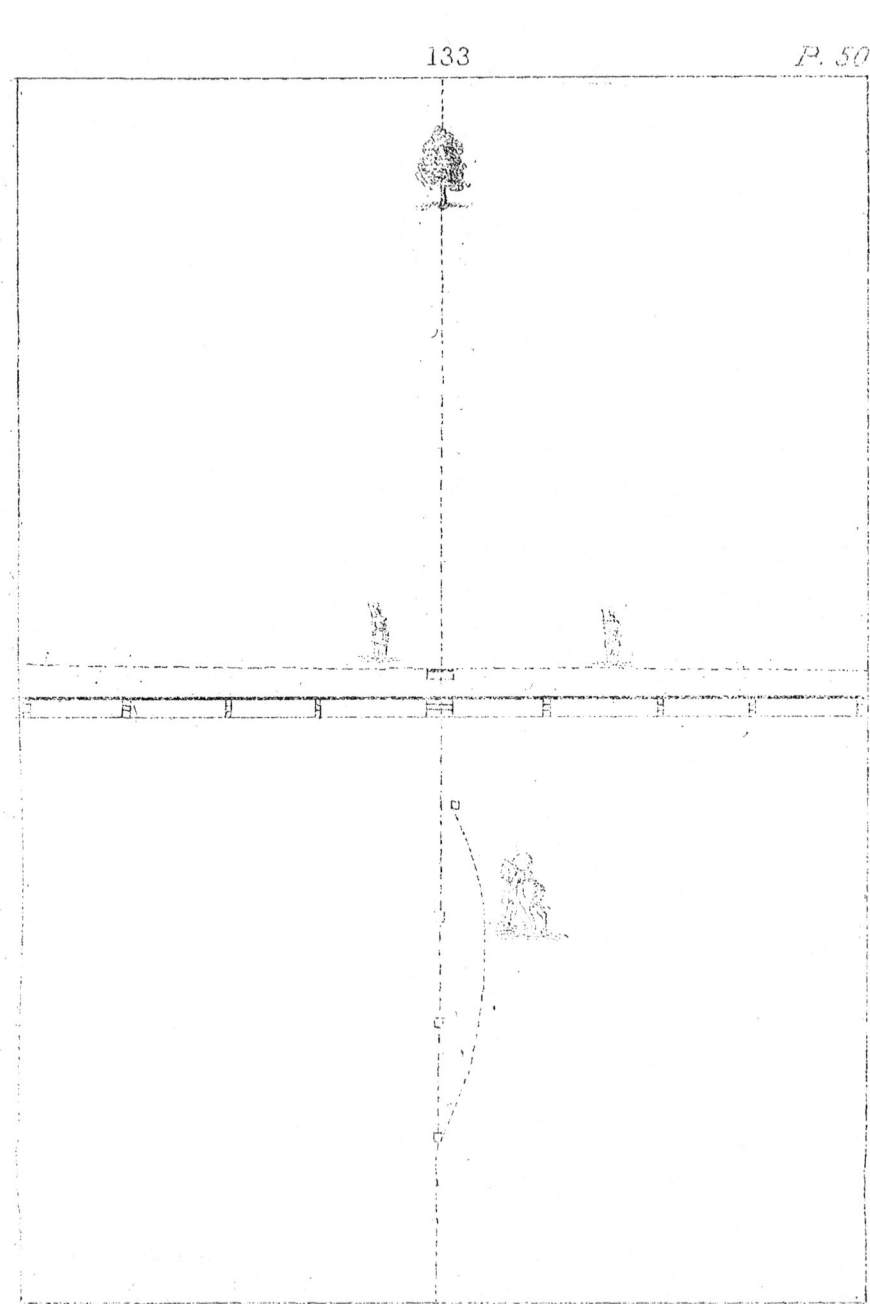

SCHOOL OF THE BATTALION—PART V. 133

rank of the battalion, and the second at the same distance from the first.

590. The color-bearer will be instructed to take, the moment the lieutenant colonel shall be established on the perpendicular, two points on the ground in the straight line which, drawn from himself, would pass between the heels of that officer; the first of these points will be taken at fifteen or twenty paces from the color-bearer.

591. These dispositions being made, the colonel will command:

1. *Battalion, forward.*

592. At this, the front rank of the color-guard will advance six paces to the front; the corporals in the rear rank will place themselves in the front rank, and these will be replaced by those in the rank of file closers; at the same time the two general guides will move in advance, abreast with the color-bearer, the one on the right, opposite to the captain of the right company, the other opposite to the sergeant who closes the left of the battalion.

593. The captains of the left wing will shift, passing before the front rank, to the left of their respective companies; the sergeant on the left of the battalion will step back into the rear rank. The covering sergeant of the company next on the left of the color-company, will step into the front rank.

594. The lieutenant colonel having assured the color-bearer on the line between himself and the corporal of the color-file, now in the front rank,
VOL. II.—12

will go to the position which will be hereinafter indicated, No. 602.

595. The major will place himself six or eight paces on either flank of the color-rank.

596. The colonel will then command:

2. MARCH (or *double quick*—MARCH).

597. At this command, the battalion will step off with life; the color-bearer, charged with the step and direction, will scrupulously observe the length and cadence of the pace, marching on the prolongation of the two points previously taken, and successively taking others in advance by the means indicated in the school of the company; the corporal on his right, and the one on his left, will march in the same step, taking care not to turn the head or shoulders, the color-bearer supporting the color-lance against the hip.

598. The two general guides will march in the same step with the color-rank, each maintaining himself abreast, or nearly so, with that rank, and neither occupying himself with the movement of the other.

599. The three corporals of the color-guard, now in the front rank of the battalion, will march well aligned, elbow to elbow, heads direct to the front, and without deranging the line of their shoulders; the centre one will follow exactly in the trace of the color-bearer, and maintain the same step, without lengthening or shortening it, except on an intimation from the colonel or lieutenant colonel, although he should find himself more or less than six paces from the color-rank.

600. The covering sergeant in the front rank between the color-company and the next on the left, will march elbow to elbow, and on the same line, with the three corporals in the centre, his head well to the front.

601. The captains of the color-company, and the company next to the left, will constitute, with the three corporals in the centre of the front rank, the basis of alignment for both wings of the battalion; they will march in the same step with the color-bearer, and exert themselves to maintain their shoulders exactly in the square with the direction. To this end, they will keep their heads direct to the front, only occasionally casting an eye on the three centre corporals, with the slightest possible turn of the neck, and if they perceive themselves in advance, or in rear of these corporals, the captain, or two captains, will almost insensibly shorten or lengthen the step, so as, at the end of several paces, to regain the true alignment, without giving sudden checks or impulsions to the wings beyond them respectively.

602. The lieutenant colonel, placed twelve or fifteen paces on the right of the captain of the color-company, will maintain this captain and the next one beyond, abreast with the three centre corporals; to this end, he will caution either to lengthen or to shorten the step as may be necessary, which the captain, or two captains, will execute as has just been explained.

603. All the other captains will maintain themselves on the prolongation of this basis; and, to this end, they will cast their eyes towards the cen-

tre, taking care to turn the neck but slightly, and not to derange the direction of their shoulders.

604. The captains will observe the march of their companies, and prevent the men from getting in advance of the line of captains; they will not lengthen or shorten step except when evidently necessary; because, to correct, with too scrupulous attention, small faults, is apt to cause the production of greater — loss of calmness, silence, and equality of step, each of which it is so important to maintain.

605. The men will constantly keep their heads well directed to the front, feel lightly the elbow towards the centre, resist pressure coming from the flank, give the greatest attention to the squareness of shoulders, and hold themselves always very slightly behind the line of the captains, in order never to shut out from the view of the latter the basis of alignment; they will, from time to time, cast an eye on the color-rank, or on the general guide of the wing, in order to march constantly in the same step with those advanced persons.

606. Pending the march, the line determined by the two markers (h and d) will be prolonged by placing, in proportion as the battalion advances, a third marker (i) in the rear of the first (h), then the marker (d) will quit his place and go a like distance in rear of (i); the marker (h) will, in his turn, do the like in respect to (d), and so on, in succession, as long as the battalion continues to advance; each marker, on shifting position, taking care to face to the rear, and to cover accurately the two markers already established on the direction. A staff officer, or the quartermaster sergeant, de-

137

signated for the purpose, and who will hold himself constantly fifteen or twenty paces facing the marker farthest from the battalion, will caution each marker when to shift place, and assure him on the direction behind the other two.

607. The colonel will habitually hold himself about thirty paces in rear of the centre of his battalion, taking care not to put himself on the line of markers; if, for example, by the slanting of the battalion, or the indications which will be given, Nos. 617 and following, he find that the march of the color-bearer is not perpendicular, he will promptly command:

Point of direction to the right (or *left*).

608. At this command, the major will hasten thirty or forty paces in advance of the color-rank, halt, face to the colonel, and place himself on the direction which the latter will indicate by signal of the sword; the corporal in the centre of the battalion will then direct himself upon the major, on a caution from the colonel, advancing, to that end, the opposite shoulder; the corporals on his right and left will conform themselves to his direction.

609. The color-bearer will also direct himself upon the major, advancing the opposite shoulder, the major causing him, at the same time, to incline to the right or left, until he shall exactly cover the corporal of his file; the color-bearer will then take points on the ground in this new direction.

610. The two general guides will conform themselves to the new direction of the color-rank.

611. The officer charged with observing the successive replacing of the markers in the rear of the centre, will establish them promptly on the new direction, taking for basis the color-bearer and the corporal of his file in the centre of the battalion; the colonel will verify the new direction of the markers.

612. The lieutenant colonel, from the position given, No. 602, will see that the two centre companies, and successively all the others, conform themselves to the new direction of the centre, but without precipitancy or disorder; he will then endeavor to maintain that basis of alignment for the battalion, perpendicularly to the direction pursued by the color-bearer.

613. He will often observe the march of the two wings; and, if he discover that the captains neglect to conform themselves to the basis of alignment, he will recall their attention by the command — *captain of* (such) *company,* or *captains of* (such) *companies, on the line* — without, however, endeavoring too scrupulously to correct small faults.

614. The major on the flank of the color-rank will, during the march, place himself, from time to time, twenty paces in front of that rank, face to the rear, and place himself correctly on the prolongation of the markers established behind the centre, in order to verify the exact march of the color-bearer on that line; he will rectify, if necessary, the direction of the color-bearer, who will

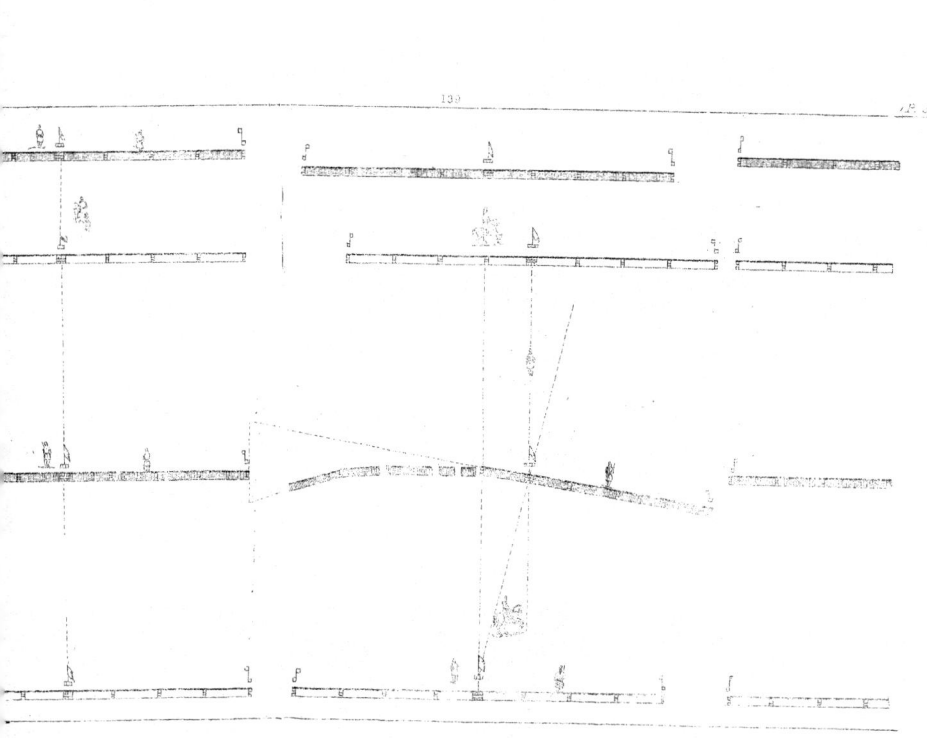

immediately take two new points on the ground between himself and the major.

615. All the principles applicable to the advance in line, are the same for a *subordinate* as for the *directing* battalion ; but when the battalion under instruction is supposed to be *subordinate,* no markers will be placed behind its centre.

Remarks on the advance in line of battle.

616. If, in the exercises of detail, or courses of elementary instruction, the officers, sergeants, corporals, and men, have not been well confirmed in the principles of the position under arms, as well as in the length and cadence of the step, the march of the battalion in line will be floating, unsteady, and disunited.

617. If the color-bearer, instead of marching perpendicularly forward, pursue an oblique direction, the battalion will slant; crowdings in one wing, and openings in the other, will follow, and these defects in the march, becoming more and more embarrassing in proportion to the deviation from the perpendicular, will commence near the centre.

618. It is then of the greatest importance that the color-bearer should direct himself perpendicularly forward, and that the basis of alignment should always be perpendicular to the line pursued by him.

619. If openings be formed, if the files crowd each other, if, in short, disorder ensue, the remedy ought to be applied as promptly as possible.

but calmly, with few words, and as little noise as practicable.

620. The object of the general guides, in the march in line of battle is, to indicate to the companies near the flanks the step of the centre of the battalion, and to afford more facility in establishing the wings on the direction of the centre if they should be too much in the rear; hence the necessity that these guides should maintain the same step, and march abreast, or very nearly so, with the color-rank, which it will be easy for them to do by casting from time to time an eye on that rank.

621. If the battalion happen to lose the step, the colonel will recall its attention by the command, *to the*—STEP; captains and their companies will immediately cast an eye on the color-rank, or one of the general guides, and promptly conform themselves to the step.

622. Finally, it is of the utmost importance to the attainment of regularity in the march in line of battle, to habituate the battalion to execute with as much order as promptness the movements prescribed No. 607 and following, for rectifying the direction; it is not less essential that commanders of battalions should exercise themselves, with the greatest care, in forming their own *coup d'œil*, in order to be able to judge with precision the direction to be given to their battalions.

Article Second.

Oblique march in line of battle.

623. The battalion marching in line of battle, when the colonel shall wish to cause it to oblique, he will command:

1. *Right* (or *left*) *oblique.* 2. March (or *double quick*—March).

624. At the first command, the major will place himself in front of, and faced to the color-bearer.

625. At the command *march*, the whole battalion will take the oblique step. The companies and captains will strictly observe the principles established in the school of the company.

626. The major in front of the color-bearer ought to maintain the latter in a line with the centre corporal, so that the color-bearer may oblique neither more nor less than that corporal. He will carefully observe also that they follow parallel directions and preserve the same length of step.

627. The lieutenant colonel will take care that the captains and the three corporals in the centre keep exactly on a line and follow parallel directions.

628. The colonel will see that the battalion preserves its parallelism; he will exert himself to prevent the files from opening or crowding. If he perceive the latter fault, he will cause the files on the flank, to which the battalion obliques, to open out.

629. The colonel, wishing the direct march to be resumed, will command:

1. *Forward.* 2. March.

630. At the command *march*, the battalion will resume the direct march. The major will place himself thirty paces in front of the color-bearer, and face to the colonel, who will establish him, by a signal of the sword, on the direction which the color-bearer ought to pursue. The latter will immediately take two points on the ground between himself and the major.

631. In resuming the direct march, care will be taken that the men do not close the intervals which may exist between the files at once; it should be done almost insensibly.

Remarks on the oblique march.

632. The object of the oblique step is to gain ground to the right or left, preserving all the while the primitive direction of the line of battle; as thus, for example: the battalion, departing from the line (sz), arrives on the line (xx) parallel to (sz).

633. It is then essential that the corporals in the centre of the battalion, and the captains of companies, should follow parallel directions, and maintain themselves at the same height; without which they will give a false direction to the battalion.

634. The colonel and lieutenant colonel will exert themselves to prevent the files from crowding; for, without such precaution, the oblique march cannot be executed with facility.

Article Third.

To halt the battalion, marching in line of battle, and to align it.

635. The battalion, marching in the line of battle, when the colonel shall wish to halt it, he will command:

1. *Battalion.* 2. Halt.

636. At the second command, the battalion will halt; the color-rank and the general guides will remain in front; but if the colonel should not wish immediately to resume the advance in line, nor to give a general alignment, he will command:

Color and general guides—Posts.

637. At this command, the color-rank and general guides will retake their places in line of battle, the captains in the left wing will shift to the right of their companies.

638. If the colonel should then judge it necessary to rectify the alignment, he will command:

Captains, rectify the alignment.

639. The captains will immediately cast an eye towards the centre, align themselves accurately, on the basis of the alignment, which the lieutenant colonel will see well directed, and then promptly dress their respective companies. The

lieutenant colonel will admonish such captains as may not be accurately on the alignment by the command: *Captain of* (such) *company*, or *captains of* (such) *companies, move up or fall back.*

640. But when the colonel shall wish to give the battalion a general alignment, either parallel or oblique, instead of rectifying it as above, he will move some paces outside of one of the general guides (the right will here be supposed) and caution the right general guide and the color-bearer to face him, and then establish them by signal of the sword, on the direction which he may wish to give to the battalion. As soon as they shall be correctly established, the left general guide will place himself on their direction, and be assured in his position by the major. The color-bearer will carry the color-lance perpendicularly between his eyes, and the two corporals of his rank will return to their places in the front rank the moment he shall face to the colonel.

641. This disposition being made, the colonel will command:

1. *Guides*—On the Line.

642. At this command, the right guide of each company in the right wing, and the left guide of each company in the left, will each place himself on the direction of the color-bearer and the two general guides, face to the color-bearer, place himself in rear of the guide who is next before him at a distance equal to the front of his company, and align himself upon the color-bearer and the general guide beyond.

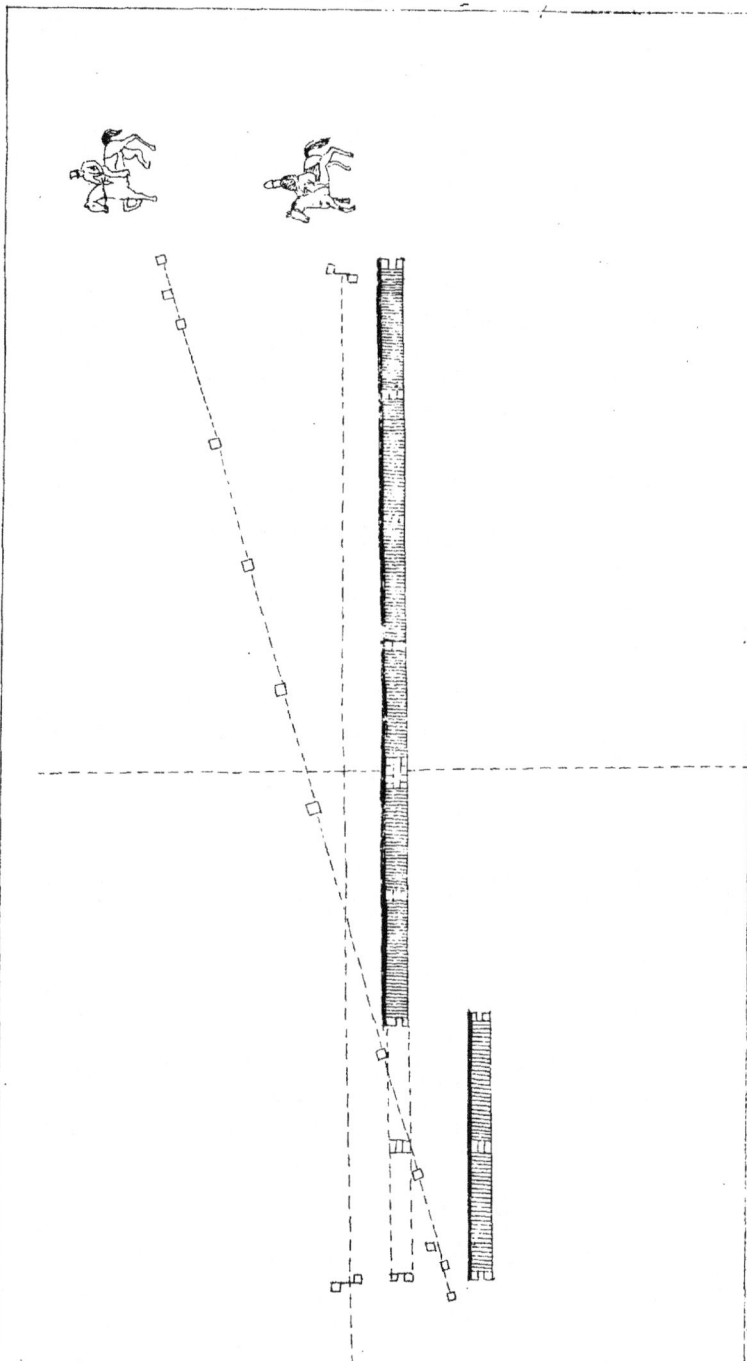

SCHOOL OF THE BATTALION—PART V. 145

643. The captains in the right wing will shift to the left of their companies, except the captain of the color-company, who will remain on its right, but step into the rear rank; the captains in the left wing will shift to the right of their companies.

644. The lieutenant colonel will promptly rectify, if necessary, the positions of the guides of the right wing, and the major those of the other; which being executed, the colonel will command:

2. *On the centre*—DRESS.

645. At this command, the companies will move up in quick time against the guides, where, having arrived, each captain will align his company according to prescribed principles, the lieutenant colonel aligning the color-company.

646. If the alignment be oblique, the captains will take care to conform their companies to it in conducting them towards the line.

647. The battalion being aligned, the colonel will command:

3. *Color and guides*—POSTS.

648. At this command, the color-bearer, the general and company guides, and the captains in the right wing, will take their places in the line of battle, and the color-bearer will replace the heel of the color-lance against the right hip.

649. If the new direction of the line of battle be such that one or more companies find themselves in advance of that line, the colonel, before establishing the general guides on the line, will cause such

VOL. II.—13 K

companies to be moved to the rear, either by the back step, or by first facing about, according as there may be less or more ground to be repassed to bring the companies in rear of the new direction.

650. When the colonel shall wish to give a general alignment, and the color and general guides are not on the line, he will cause them to move out by the command:

1. *Color and general guides*—On the Line.

651. At this command, the color-bearer and the general guides will place themselves on the line, conforming to what is prescribed, No. 640.

Article Fourth.

Change of direction in marching in line of battle.

652. The battalion marching in line of battle, when the colonel shall wish it to change direction to the right, he will command:

1. *Change direction to the right.* 2. March (or double quick—March).

653. At the command *march*, the movement will commence; the color-rank will shorten the step to fourteen or seventeen inches, and direct itself circularly to the right, taking care to advance the left shoulder, but only insensibly; the major will place himself before the color-bearer, facing him,

146

P. 54

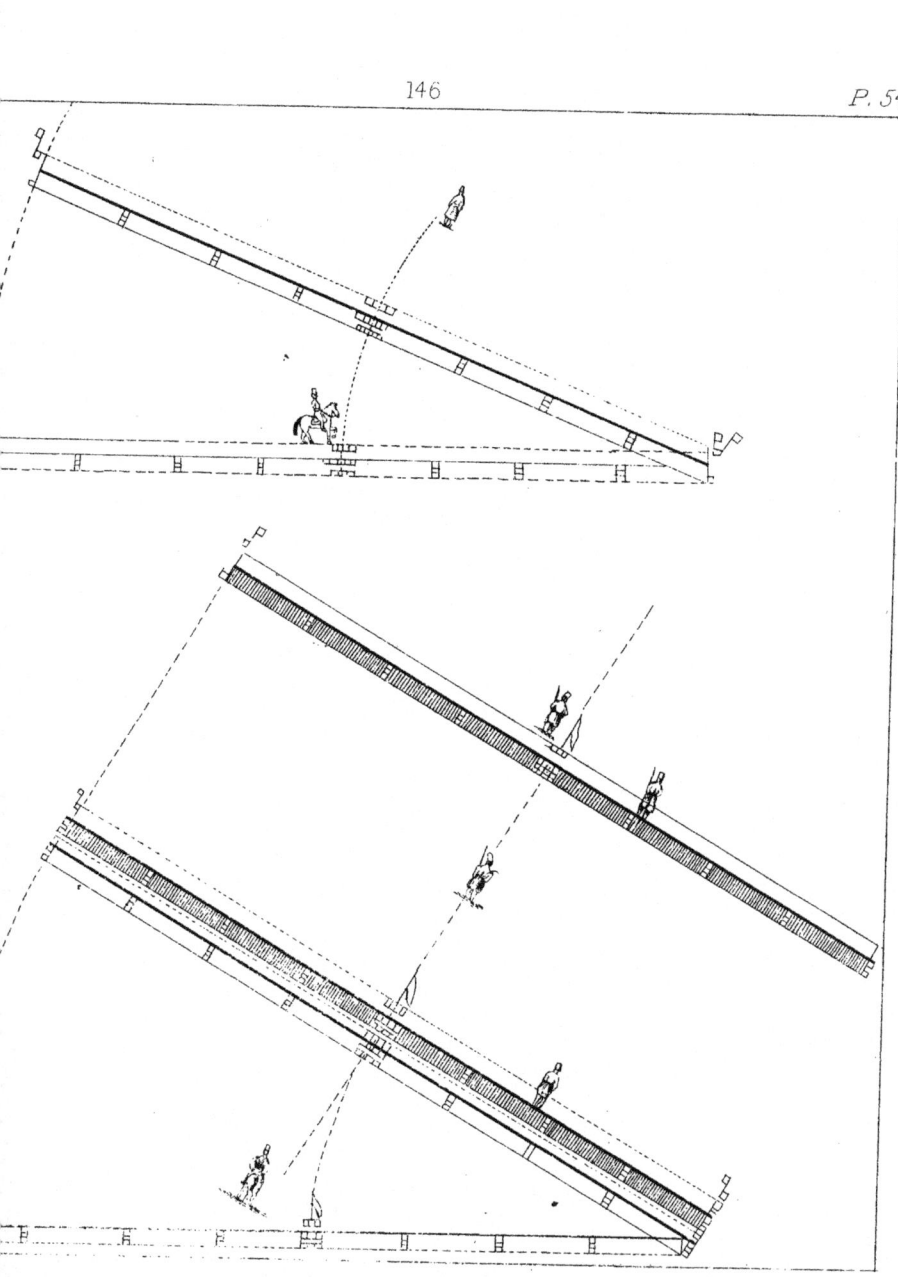

SCHOOL OF THE BATTALION—PART V. 147

and so direct his march that he may describe an arc of a circle neither too large nor too small; he will also see that the color-bearer takes steps of fourteen or seventeen inches, according to the gait.

654. The right general guide will wheel on the right captain of the battalion as his pivot; the left general guide will circularly march in the step of twenty-eight inches or thirty-three inches, according to the gait, and will align himself upon the color-bearer and the right general guide.

655. The corporal placed in the centre of the battalion, will take steps of fourteen or seventeen inches, and will wheel to the right by advancing insensibly the left shoulder; the battalion will conform itself to the movement of the centre; to this end, the captain of the color-company, and the captain of the next to the left, will attentively regulate their march, as well as the direction of their shoulders, on the three centre corporals. All the other captains will regulate the direction of their shoulders and the length of their step on this basis.

656. The men will redouble their attention in order not to pass the line of captains.

657. In the left wing, the pace will be lengthened in proportion as the file is distant from the centre; the captain of the eighth company who closes the left flank of the battalion will take steps of twenty-eight or thirty-three inches, according to the gait.

658. In the right wing the pace will be shortened in proportion as the file is distant from the centre; the captain who closes the right flank will only

slowly turn in his person, observing to yield ground a little if pushed.

659. The colonel will take great care to prevent the centre of the battalion from describing an arc of a circle, either too great or too small, in order that the wings may conform themselves to its movement. He will see also that the captains keep their companies constantly aligned upon the centre, so that there may be no opening and no crowding of files. He will endeavor to prevent faults, and, should they occur, correct them without noise.

660. The lieutenant colonel, placed before the battalion, will give his attention to the same objects.

661. When the colonel shall wish the direct march to be resumed, he will command:

1. *Forward.* 2. March.

662. At the command *march*, the color-rank, the general guides, and the battalion will resume the direct march; the major will immediately place himself thirty or forty paces in front, face to the colonel, placed in rear of the centre, who will establish him by signal of the sword on the perpendicular direction which the corporal in the centre of the battalion ought to pursue; the major will immediately cause the color-bearer, if necessary, to incline to the right or left, so as to be exactly opposite to his file; the color-bearer will then take two points on the ground between himself and the major.

663. The lieutenant colonel will endeavor to give

to the color-company and the next on the left a direction perpendicular to that pursued by the centre corporal; and all the other companies, without precipitancy, will conform themselves to that basis.

Article Fifth.

To march in retreat, in line of battle.

664. The battalion being halted, if it be the wish of the colonel to cause it to march in retreat, he will command:

1. *Face to the rear.* 2. *Battalion, about*—Face.

665. At the second command, the battalion will face about; the color-rank, and the general guides, if in advance, will take their places in line; the color-bearer will pass into the rear rank, now leading; the corporal of his file will step behind the corporal next on his own right, to let the color-bearer pass, and then step into the front rank, now rear, to re-form the color-file; the colonel will place himself behind the front rank, become the rear; the lieutenant colonel and major will place themselves before the rear rank, now leading.

666. Tne colonel will take post forty paces behind the color-file, in order to assure the lieutenant colonel on the perpendicular, who will place himself at a like distance in front, as prescribed for the advance in line of battle.

667. If the battalion be the one charged with the direction, the colonel will establish markers in

13 *

the manner indicated, No. 589, except that they will face to the battalion, and that the first will be placed twenty-five paces from the lieutenant colonel. If the markers be already established, the officer charged with replacing them in succession will cause them to face about, the moment that the battalion executes this movement, and then the marker nearest to the battalion will hasten to the rear of the two others.

668. These dispositions being made, the colonel will command:

3. *Battalion, forward.*

669. At this command, the color-bearer will advance six paces beyond the rank of file closers, accompanied by the two corporals of his guard of that rank, the centre corporal stepping back to let the color-bearer pass; the two file closers nearest this centre corporal will unite on him behind the color-guard to serve as a basis of alignment for the line of file closers; the two general guides will place themselves abreast with the color rank, the covering sergeants will place themselves in the line of file closers, and the captains in the rear rank, now leading; the captains in the left wing, now right, will, if not already there, shift to the left of their companies, now become the right.

670. The colonel will then command:

4. MARCH (or *double quick*—MARCH).

671. The battalion will march in retreat on the same principles which govern the advance in line:

the centre corporal behind the color-bearer will march exactly in his trace.

672. If it be the directing battalion, the color-bearer will direct himself on the markers, who will, of their own accord, each place himself in succession behind the marker most distant, on being approached by the battalion: the officer charged with the superintendence of the markers, will carefully assure them on the direction.

673. In the case of a subordinate battalion, the color-bearer will maintain himself on the perpendicular by means of points taken on the ground.

674. The colonel, lieutenant colonel, and major will each discharge the same functions as in the advance in line.

675. The lieutenant colonel, placed on the outside of the file closers of the color-company, will also maintain the three file closers of the basis of alignment in a square with the line of direction: the other file closers will keep themselves aligned on this basis.

Article Sixth.

To halt the battalion marching in retreat, and to face it to the front.

676. The colonel having halted the battalion, and wishing to face it to the front, will command:

1. *Face to the front.* 2. *Battalion, about*—Face.

677. At the second command, the color-rank,

general guides, captains, and covering sergeants, will all retake their habitual places in line of battle, and the color-bearer will repass into the front rank.

678. The battalion marching in line of battle by the front rank, when the colonel shall wish to march it in retreat, he will command:

1. *Battalion, right about.* 2. MARCH.

679. At the command *march*, the battalion will face to the rear and move off at the same gait by the rear rank. The principles prescribed Nos. 669 and following will be carefully observed.

680. If the colonel should wish the battalion to march again by the front, he will give the same commands.

ARTICLE SEVENTH.

Change of direction, in marching in retreat.

681. A battalion retiring in line will change direction by the commands and means indicated No. 652 and following; the three file closers, united behind the color-rank, will conform themselves to the movement of this rank, and wheel like it; the centre file closer of the three will take steps of fourteen or seventeen inches, according to the gait, and keep himself steadily at the same distance from the color-bearer; the line of file closers will conform themselves to the movement of its centre, and the lieutenant colonel will maintain it on that basis.

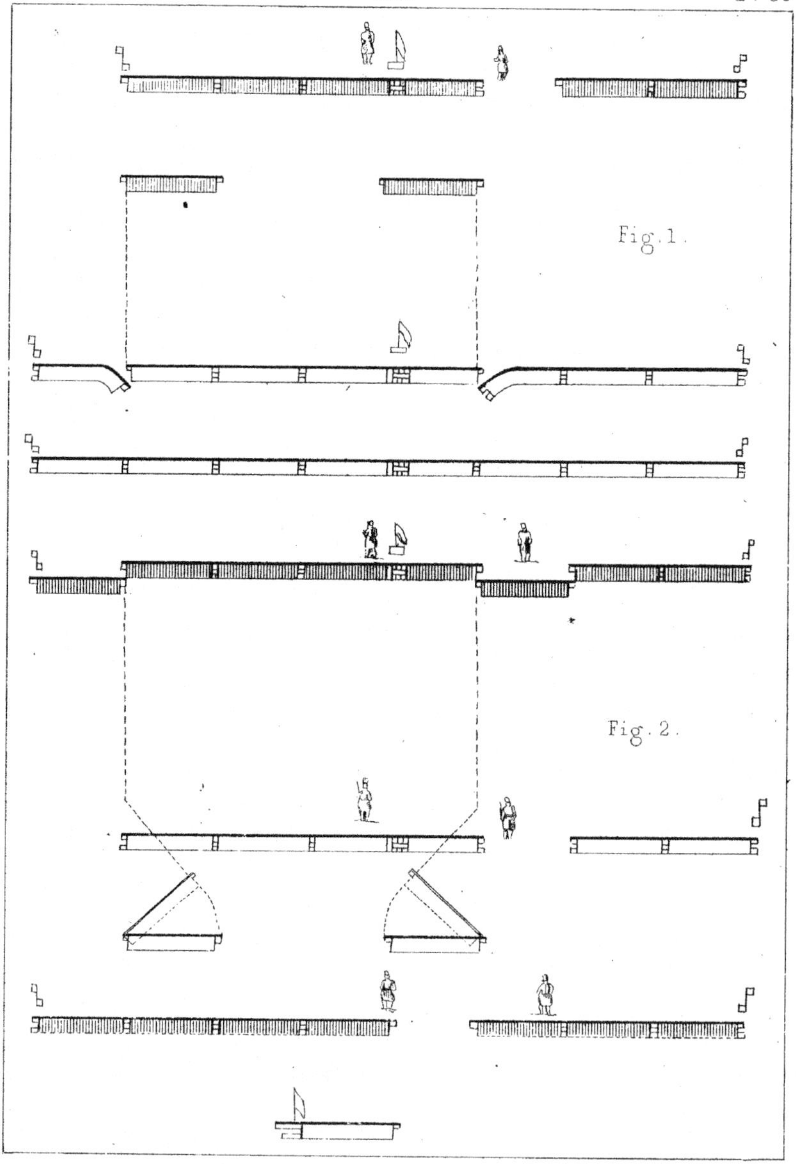

153

Fig. 1.

Fig. 2.

Article Eighth.

Passage of obstacles, advancing and retreating.

682. The battalion advancing in line will be supposed to encounter an obstacle which covers one or more companies; the colonel will cause them to ploy into column at full distance, in rear of the next company towards the color, which will be executed in the following manner. It will be supposed that the obstacle only covers the third company, the colonel will command:

Third company, obstacle.

683. At this command, the captain of the third company will place himself in its front, turn to it, and command, 1. *Third company, by the left flank, to the rear into column.* 2. *Double quick.* 3. March. He will then hasten to the left of his company.

684. At the command *march*, the company will face to the left in marching; the two left files will promptly disengage to the rear in double quick time; the left guide, placing himself at the head of the front rank, will conduct it behind the fourth company, directing himself parallelly with this company; the captain of the third will himself halt opposite to the captain of the fourth, and see his company file past; when its right file shall be nearly up with him, he will command, 1. *Third company.* 2. *By the right flank.* 3. March. 4. *Guide right*, and place himself before the centre of his company.

685. At the command *march*, the company will face to the right, preserving the same gait, but the moment it shall be at the prescribed distance, its captain will command:

1. *Quick time.* 2. March.

686. This company will thus follow in column that behind which it finds itself, and at wheeling distance, its right guide marching exactly in the trace of the captain of that company.

687. As soon as the third company shall have faced to the left, the left guide of the second will place himself on the left of the front rank of his company, and maintain between himself and the right of the fourth the space necessary for the return into line of the third.

688. The obstacle being passed, the colonel will command:

Third company, forward, into line.

689. At this command, the captain turning to his company, will add:

1. *By company, right half wheel.* 2. *Double quick.* 3. March.

690. At the command *march*, the company will take the double quick step, and execute a half wheel; its captain will then command, 1. *Forward.* 2. March. 3. *Guide left.* The second command will be given when the company shall have sufficiently wheeled.

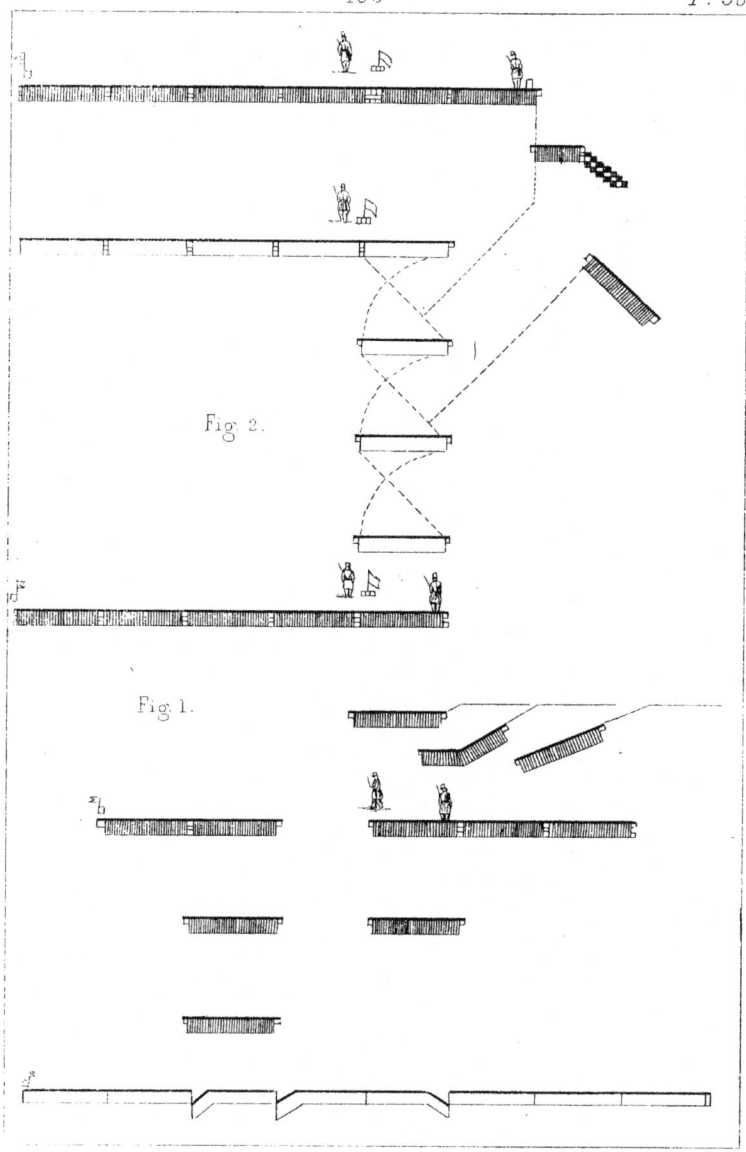

691. At the command *march*, the company will direct itself straight forward towards the line of battle, and retake its position in it according to the principles prescribed for the formation forward into line of battle.

692. It will be supposed that the obstacle covers several contiguous companies (the three companies on the right for example), the colonel will command:

1. *Three right companies, obstacle.* 2. *By the left flank, to the rear, into column.* 3. *Double quick—* MARCH.

693. At the first command, the captains of the designated companies will each place himself before the centre of his company, and caution it as to the movement about to be executed.

694. At the command *march*, the designated companies will face to the left in marching, and immediately take the double quick step; each captain will cause the head of his company to disengage itself to the rear, and the left guide will place himself at the head of the front rank; the captain of the third company will conform himself to what is prescribed, No. 684 and following; the captains of the other companies will conduct them by the flank in rear of the third, inclining towards the head of the column; and, as the head of each company arrives opposite to the right of the one next before it in column, its captain will himself halt, see his company file past, and conform himself for facing it to the front, in marching, to what is prescribed No. 684 and following.

695. When the last company in column shall have passed the obstacle, the colonel will command:

1. *Three right companies, forward, into line.*

696. At this command, the captain of each of these three companies will command, *By company, right half wheel.* The colonel will then add:

1. *Double quick.* 2. March.

697. At this, briskly repeated by the captains of the three companies, each company will conform itself to what is prescribed No. 690 and following.

698. It is supposed, in the foregoing examples, that the companies belonged to the right wing; if they make part of the other, they will execute the passage of an obstacle according to the same principles and by inverse means.

699. When flank companies are broken off to pass an obstacle, the general guide on that flank will place himself six paces in front of the outer file of the nearest company to him remaining in line.

700. In the preceding movements, it has been supposed that the battalion was marching in quick time, but if it be marching in double quick time, and the colonel shall wish to cause several contiguous companies to break to the rear, he will first order the battalion to march in quick time; the companies will break as indicated No. 692.

SCHOOL OF THE BATTALION—PART V.

701. When the movement is completed, the colonel will order the double quick step to be resumed. He will also cause the battalion to march in quick time when he shall wish to bring into line the several companies which are to the rear in column; the movement will be executed as previously indicated; and when the last company shall have nearly completed its movement, the colonel will cause the double quick step to be resumed.

702. In the movement of a single company, or of several companies not contiguous to each other, the battalion will continue to march in double quick time, but in these cases the companies which are to ploy into column, or re-enter the line, will increase the gait.

703. In the march in retreat, these several movements will be executed on the same principles as if the battalion marched by the front rank.

704. When a battalion, advancing in line of battle, shall be obliged to execute the right about in order to retreat, if there be companies in column, behind the rear rank, these companies will also execute the right about, put themselves in march, at the same time with the battalion, and will thus precede it in the retreat; they will afterwards successively put themselves into line by the oblique step, as the ground may permit.

705. If the battalion be marching in retreat in double quick time, and many contiguous companies be marching before the rear rank of the bat-

talion, the colonel will not change the gait of the battalion in causing them to re-enter into line.

706. When the color-company shall be obliged to execute the movement of passing an obstacle, the color-rank will return into line at the moment the company shall face to the left or right; the major will place himself six paces before the extremity of the company behind which the color-company marches in column, in order to give the step and the direction; he, himself, first taking the step from the battalion.

707. As soon as the color-company shall have returned into line, the front rank of the color-guard will again move out six paces in front of the battalion, and take the step from the major; the latter will immediately place himself twenty or thirty paces in front of the color-bearer, and face to the colonel placed behind the centre of the battalion, who will establish him on the perpendicular; and, as soon as he shall be assured on it, the color-bearer will instantly take two points on the ground between himself and the major.

708. It is prescribed, as a general rule, that the companies of the right wing ought to execute the movement of passing obstacles by the left flank, and the reverse for the companies of the other wing; but if the obstacle cover at once several companies of the centre, each will file into column behind that, still in line, and of the same wing, which may be the nearest to it.

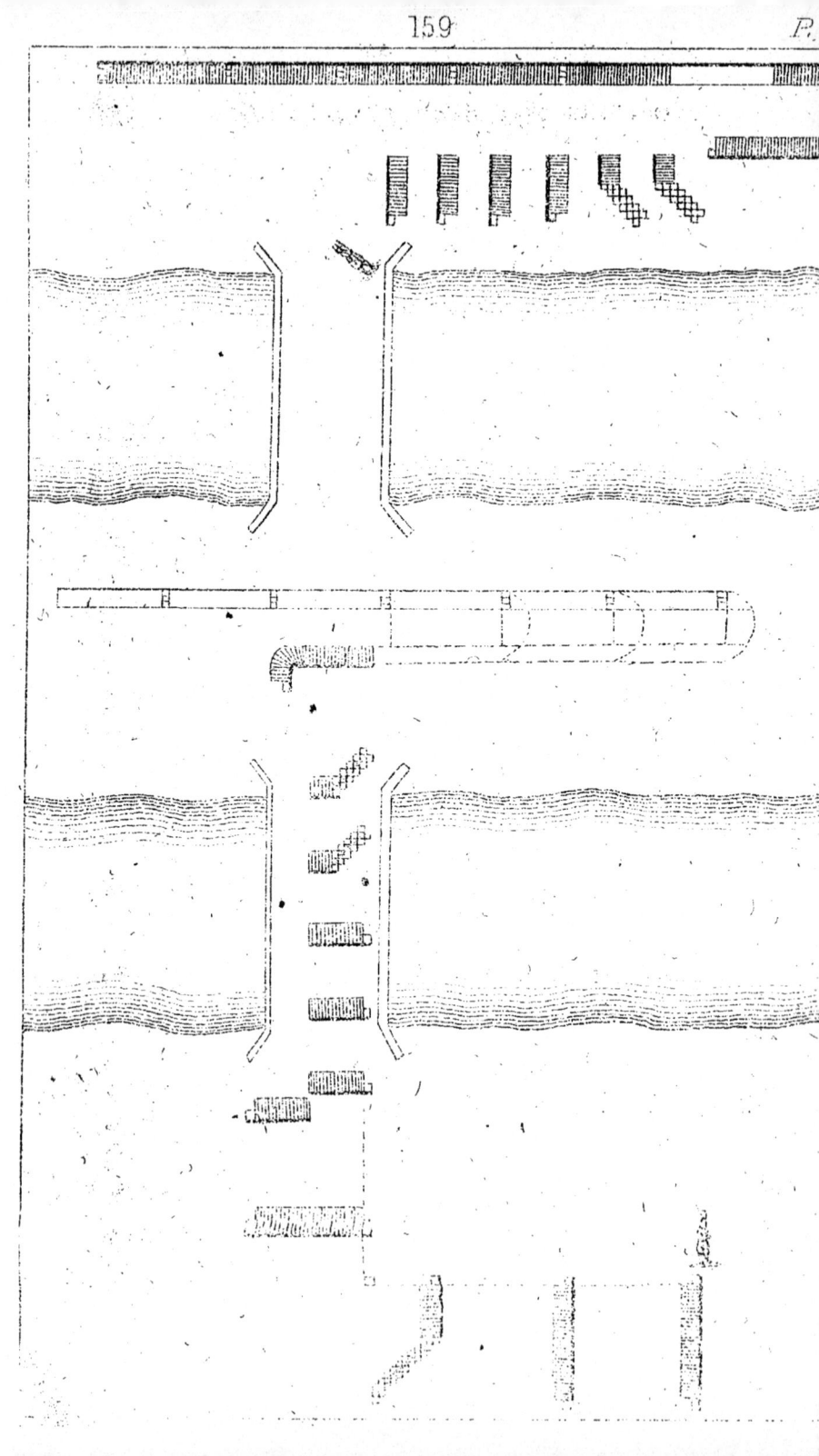

Article Ninth.

To pass a defile, in retreat, by the right or left flank.

709. When a battalion, retiring in line, shall encounter a defile which it must pass, the colonel will halt the battalion, and face it to the front.

710. It will be supposed that the defile is in rear of the left flank, and that its width is sufficient to give passage to a column by platoon; the colonel will place a marker fifteen or twenty paces in rear of the file closers at the point around which the subdivisions will have to change direction in order to enter the defile; he will then command:

To the rear, by the right flank, pass the defile.

711. The captain of the first company will immediately command:

1. *First company, right*—Face. 2. March (or double quick—March).

712. At the command *march*, the first company will commence the movement; the first file will wheel to the right, march to the rear till it shall have passed four paces beyond the file closers, when it will wheel again to the right, and then direct itself straight forward towards the left flank. All the other files of this company will

come to wheel in succession at the same place where the first had wheeled.

713. The second company will execute, in its turn, the same movement, by the commands of its captain, who will give the command MARCH, so that the first file of his company may immediately follow the last of the first, without constraint, however, as to taking the step of the first; the first file of the second company will wheel to the right, on its ground; all the other files of this company will come in succession to wheel at the same place. The following companies will execute, each in its turn, what has just been prescribed for the second.

714. When the whole of the second company shall be on the same direction with the first, the captain of the first will cause it to form, by platoon, into line, and the moment that it is in column, the guide of the first platoon will direct himself on the marker around whom he has to change direction in order to enter the defile.

715. The second company will continue to march by the flank, directing itself parallelly with the line of battle; and it, in its turn, will form by platoon into line, when the third company shall be wholly on the same direction with itself.

716. The following companies will successively execute what has just been prescribed for the second, and each will form by platoon into line, when the next company shall be on the same direction with itself.

717. The first platoon of the leading company having arrived opposite to the marker placed at the entrance of the defile, will turn to the left,

and the following platoons will all execute this movement at the same point. As the last companies will not be able to form platoons before reaching the defile, they will so direct themselves, in entering it, as to leave room to the left for this movement.

718. The battalion will thus pass the defile by platoon; and, as the two platoons of each company shall clear it, companies will be successively formed by the means indicated, school of the company, No. 273, and following.

719. The head of the column having cleared the defile, and having reached the distance at which the colonel wishes to re-form line faced to the defile, he may cause the leading company to turn to the left, to prolong the column in that direction, and then form it to the left into line of battle; or he may halt the column, and form it into line of battle faced to the rear.

720. If the defile be in the rear of the right flank, it will be passed by the left; the movement will be executed according to the same principles, and by inverse means.

721. If the defile be too narrow to receive the front of a platoon, it will be passed by the flank. Captains and file closers will be watchful that the files do not lose their distances in marching. Companies or platoons will be formed into line as the width of the defile may permit, or as the companies shall successively clear it.

Article Tenth.

To march by the flank.

722. The colonel, wishing the battalion to march by the flank, will command:

1. *Battalion.* 2. *Right* (or *left*)—Face. 3. *Forward.* 4. March (or *double quick*—March).

723. At the second command, the captains and covering sergeants will place themselves as prescribed, Nos. 136 and 141, school of the company.

724. The sergeant on the left of the battalion will place himself to the left and by the side of the last file of his company, covering the captains in file.

725. The battalion having to face by the left flank, the captains, at the second command, will shift rapidly to the left of their companies, and each place himself by the side of the covering sergeant of the company preceding his own, except the captain of the left company, who will place himself by the side of the sergeant on the left of the battalion. The covering sergeant of the right company will place himself by the right side of the front rank man of the rearmost file of his company, covering the captains in file.

726. At the command *march*, the battalion will step off with life; the sergeant, placed before the leading file (right or left in front), will be careful to preserve exactly the length and cadence of the

step, and to direct himself straight forward; to this end, he will take points on the ground.

727. Whether the battalion march by the right or left flank, the lieutenant colonel will place himself abreast with the leading file, and the major abreast with the color-file, both on the side of the front rank, and about six paces from it.

728. The adjutant, placed between the lieutenant colonel and the front rank, will march in the same step with the head of the battalion, and the sergeant major, placed between the major and the color-bearer, will march in the same step with the adjutant.

729. The captains and file closers will carefully see that the files neither open out, nor close too much, and that they regain insensibly their distances, if lost.

730. The colonel wishing the battalion to wheel by file, will command:

1. *By file right* (or *left*). 2. MARCH.

731. The files will wheel in succession, and all at the place where the first had wheeled, in conforming to the principles prescribed in the school of the company.

732. The battalion marching by the flank, when the colonel shall wish it to halt, he will command:

1. *Battalion.* 2. HALT. 3. FRONT.

733. These commands will be executed as prescribed in the school of the company, No. 146.

734. If the battalion be marching by the flank and the colonel should wish to cause it to march in line, either to the front or to the rear, the movements will be executed by the commands and means prescribed in the school of the company.

Article Eleventh.

To form the battalion on the right or left, by file, into line of battle.

735. The battalion marching by the right flank, when the colonel shall wish to form it on the right by file, he will determine the line of battle, and the lieutenant colonel will place two markers on that line, in conformity with what is prescribed, No. 415.

736. The head of the battalion being nearly up with the first marker, the colonel will command:

1. **On the right, by file, into line.** 2. **March** (or *double quick*—**March**).

737. At the command *march*, the leading company will form itself on the right, by file, into line of battle, as indicated in the school of the company, No. 149; the front rank man of the first file will rest his breast lightly against the right arm of the first marker; the other companies will follow the movement of the leading company; each captain will place himself on the line at the same **time with** the front rank man of his first file, and **on the** right of this man.

738. The left guide of each company, except the leading one, will place himself on the direction of the markers, and opposite to the left file of his company, at the instant that the front rank man of this file arrives on the line.

739. The formation being ended, the colonel will command:

Guides—Posts.

740. The colonel will superintend the successive formation of the battalion, moving along the front of the line of battle.

741. The lieutenant colonel will, in succession, assure the direction of the guides, and see that the men of the front rank, in placing themselves on the line, do not pass it.

742. If the battalion march by the left flank, the movement will be executed according to the same principles, and by inverse means.

Article Twelfth.

Changes of front.

Change of front perpendicularly forward.

743. The battalion being in line of battle, it is supposed to be the wish of the colonel to cause a change of front forward on the right company, and that the angle formed by the old and new positions be a right angle, or a few degrees more or less than one; he will cause two markers to be placed on the new direction, before the position to

be occupied by that company, and order its captain to establish it against the markers.

744. The captain of the right company will immediately direct it upon the markers by a wheel to the right on the fixed pivot; and after having halted it, he will align it by the right.

745. These dispositions being made, the colonel will command:

1. *Change front forward on first company.* 2. *By company, right half wheel.* 3. March (or *double quick*—March).

746. At the second command, each captain will place himself before the centre of his company.

747. At the third, each company will wheel to the right on the fixed pivot; the left guide of each will place himself on its left as soon as he shall be able to pass; and when the colonel shall judge that the companies have sufficiently wheeled, he will command:

4. *Forward.* 5. March. 6. *Guide right.*

748. At the fifth command, the companies ceasing to wheel will march straight forward; at the sixth, the men will touch elbows towards the right.

749. The right guide of the second company will march straight forward until this company shall arrive at the point where it should turn to the right; each succeeding right guide will follow the file immediately before him at the cessation of the wheel, and will march in the trace of this file

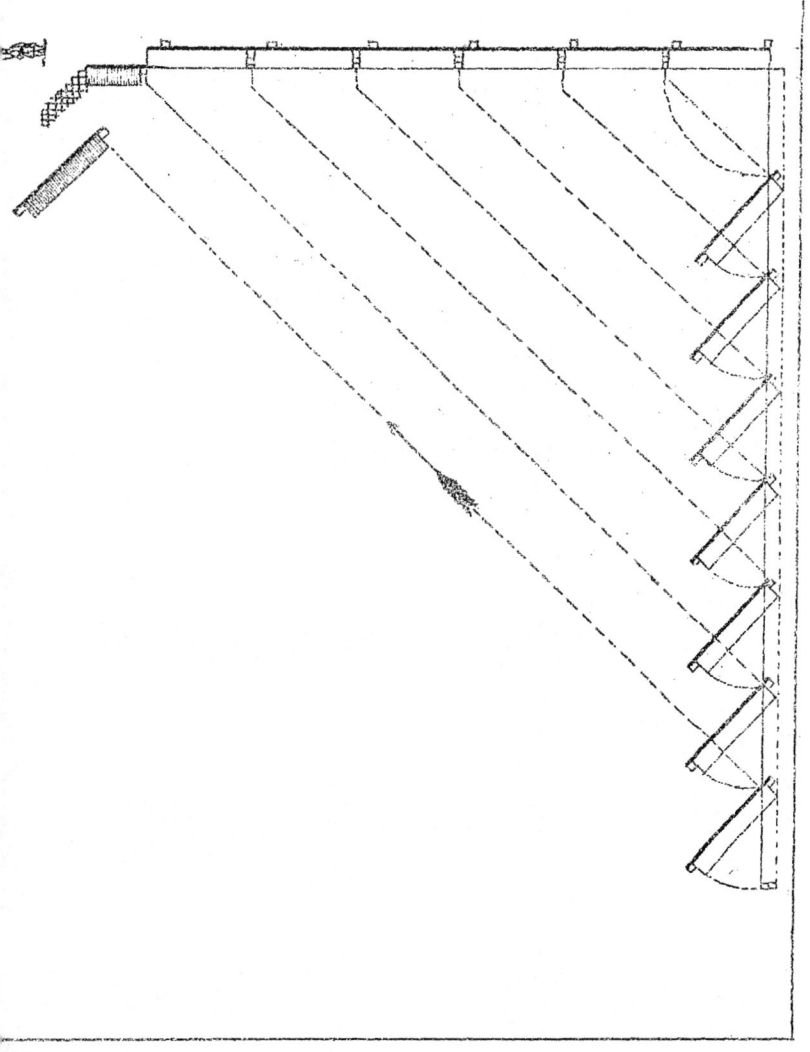

until this company shall turn to the right to move upon the line; this guide will then march straight forward.

750. The second company having arrived opposite to the left file of the first, its captain will cause it to turn to the right; the right guide will direct himself so as to arrive squarely upon the line of battle, and when he shall be at three paces from that line, the captain will command:

1. *Second company.* 2. HALT.

751. At the second command, the company will halt; the files not yet in line with the guide will come into it promptly, the left guide will place himself on the line of battle, and as soon as he is assured in the direction by the lieutenant colonel, the captain will align the company by the right.

752. Each following company will conform to what has just been prescribed for the second.

753. The formation ended, the colonel will command:

Guides—POSTS.

754. If the battalion be in march, and the colonel shall wish to change front forward on the first company, and that the angle formed by the old and new positions be a right angle, he will cause two markers to be placed on the new direction, before the position to be occupied by that company, and will command:

1. *Change front forward on first company.* 2. *By company, right half wheel.* 3. March (or *double quick*—March).

755. At the first command, the captains will move rapidly before the centre of their respective companies; the captain of the first company will command: 1. *Right turn;* 2. *Quick time;* the captains of the other companies will caution them to wheel to the right.

756. At the command *march*, the first company will turn to the right according to the principles prescribed in the school of the soldier, No. 402; its captain will halt it at three paces from the markers, and the files in rear will promptly come into line. The captain will align the company by the right.

757. Each of the other companies will wheel to the right on a fixed pivot; the left guides will place themselves on the left of their respective companies, and when the colonel shall judge they have wheeled sufficiently, he will command:

4. *Forward.* 5. March. 6. *Guide right.*

758. These commands will be executed as indicated No. 746 and following.

759. The colonel will cause the battalion to change front forward on the eighth company according to the same principles and by inverse means.

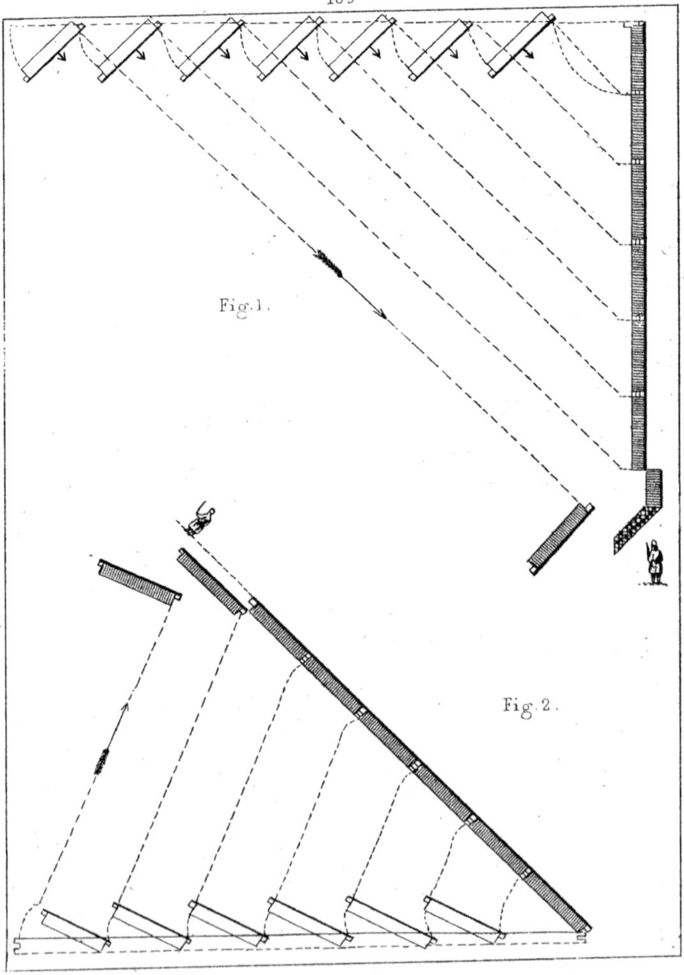

169 P. 60

Fig. 1.

Fig. 2.

SCHOOL OF THE BATTALION—PART V.

Change of front perpendicularly to the rear.

760. The colonel, wishing to change front to the rear on the right company, will impart his purpose to the captain of this company. The latter will immediately face his company about, wheel it to the left on the fixed pivot, and halt it when it shall be in the direction indicated to him by the colonel; the captain will then face his company to the front, and align it by the right against the two markers, whom the colonel will cause to be established before the right and left files.

761. These dispositions being made, the colonel will command:

1. *Change front to the rear, on first company.* 2. *Battalion, about*—FACE. 3. *By company, left half wheel.* 4. MARCH (*or double quick*—MARCH).

762. At the second command, all the companies, except the right, will face about.

763. At the third, the captains, whose companies have faced about, will each place himself behind the centre of his company, two paces from the front rank, now the rear.

764. At the fourth, these companies will wheel to the left on the fixed pivot by the rear rank; the left guide of each will, as soon as he is able to pass, place himself on the left of the rear rank of his company, now become the right; and when the colonel shall judge that the companies have sufficiently wheeled, he will command:

5. *Forward.* 6. March. 7. *Guide left.*

765. At the sixth command, the companies will cease to wheel, march straight forward towards the new line of battle, and, at the seventh, take the touch of the elbow towards the left.

766. The guide of each company on its right flank, become left, will conform himself to the principles prescribed, No. 748.

767. The second company, from the right, having arrived opposite to the left of the first, will turn to the left; the guide will so direct himself as to arrive parallelly with the line of battle, cross that line, and when the front rank, now in the rear, shall be three paces beyond it, the captain will command: 1. *Second company;* 2. Halt.

768. At the second command, the company will halt; the files which may not yet be in line with the guide, will promptly come into it; the captain will cause the company to face about, and then align it by the right.

769. All the other companies will execute what has just been prescribed for the second, each as it successively arrives opposite to the left of the company that precedes it on the new line of battle.

770. The formation being ended, the colonel will command:

Guides—Posts.

771. The colonel will cause a change of front on the left company of the battalion to the rear, according to the same principles and by inverse means.

772. In changes of front, the colonel will give a general superintendence to the movement.

773. The lieutenant colonel will assure the direction of the guides as they successively move out on the line of battle, conforming himself to what has been prescribed in the successive formations.

Remarks on changes of front.

774. When the new direction is perpendicular, or nearly so, to that of the battalion, the companies ought to make about a *half wheel* (the eighth of the circle) before marching straight forward; but when those two lines are oblique to each other, the smaller the angle which they form, the less ought the companies to wheel. It is for the colonel to judge, according to the angle, the precise time when he ought to give the command *march* after the caution *forward*, and if he cannot catch the exact moment, the word of execution should rather be given a little too soon, than an instant too late.

775. When the old and the new lines form an angle of forty-five or fewer degrees, the colonel will find it necessary to arrest the wheel of the companies when the marching flanks shall have taken but a few paces, or, it may be, have but disengaged, respectively, from the fixed pivots of the next companies; and in all such cases, the companies will arrive so nearly parallel to the new line, as to be able to align themselves upon it without the intermediate turn to the right or left:

to execute the movement under either circumstance supposed, the colonel will command:

Oblique change of front, forward (or *to the rear*) *on* (*such company*).

Article Thirteenth.

To ploy the battalion into column doubled on the centre.

776. This movement consists in ploying the corresponding companies of the right and left wings into column at company distance, or closed in mass, in rear of the two centre companies, according to the principles prescribed, Article Third, Part Second, of this School.

777. The colonel, wishing to form the double column at company distance, (the battalion being in line of battle,) will command:

1. *Double column, at half distance.* 2. *Battalion, inwards*—Face. 3. March (or *double quick*—March.)

778. At the first command, the captains will place themselves two paces in front of their respective companies; the captains of the two centre companies will caution them to stand fast, and the other captains will caution their companies to face to the left and right, respectively. The covering sergeants will step into the front rank.

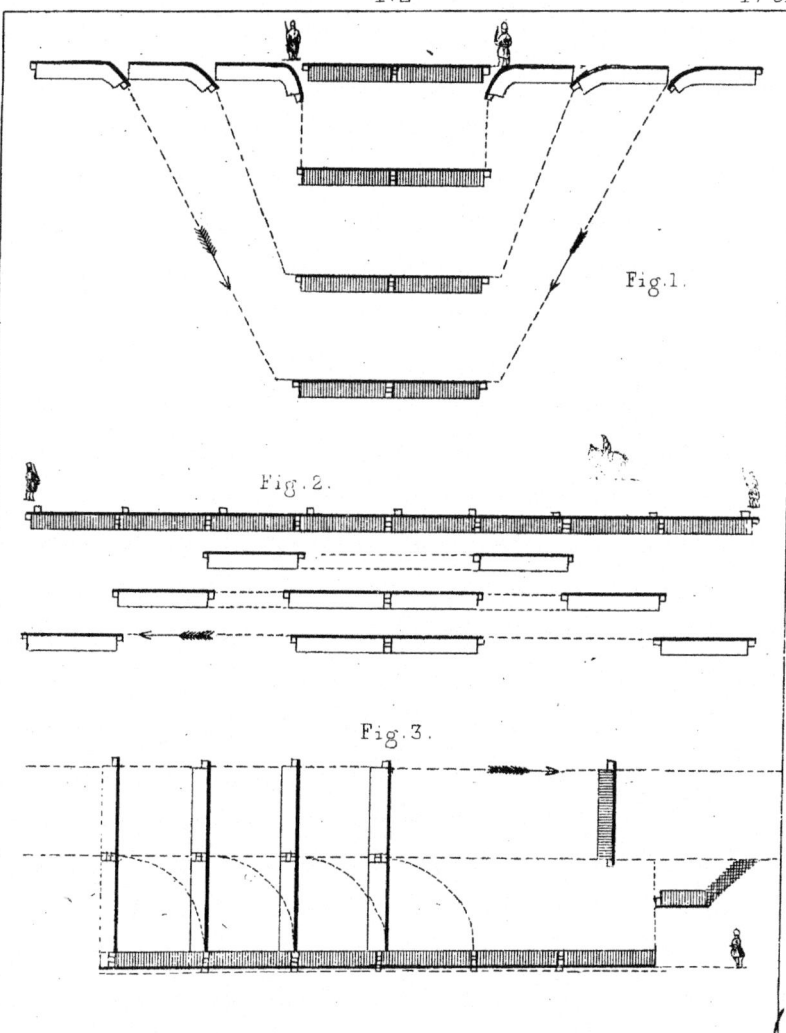

779. At the second command, the fourth and fifth companies will stand fast; the others of the right wing will face to the left, and the others of the left wing will face to the right; each captain whose company has faced, will hasten to break to the rear the two files at the head of his company; the left guide of each right company, and the right guide of each left company, will each place himself at the head of its front rank, and the captain by the side of his guide.

780. At the command *march*, the fourth and fifth companies, which are to form the first division, will stand fast; the senior captain of the two will place himself before the centre of the division, and command: *Guide right;* the junior captain will place himself in the interval between the two companies, and the left guide of the left company will place himself in the front rank on the left of the division, as soon as he shall be able to pass.

781. All the other companies, conducted by their captains, will step off with life to arrange themselves in column at company distance, each company behind the preceding one in the column of the same wing, so that, in the right wing, the third may be next behind the fourth, the second next to the third, and so on to the right company; and, in the left wing, the sixth may be next behind the fifth, the seventh next to the sixth, and so on to the left company of the battalion.

782. The corresponding companies of the two wings will unite into divisions in arranging themselves in column; an instant before the union, at the centre of the column, the left guides of right companies will pass into the line of file closers,

and each captain will command: 1. *Such company*; 2. *Halt;* 3. Front.

783. At the second command, which will be given at the instant of union, each company will halt; at the third, it will face to the front. The senior captain in each division will place himself on its right, and command, *Right*—Dress, and the junior captain will place himself in the interval between the two companies. The division being aligned, its chief will command Front, and take his position two paces before its centre.

784. The column being thus formed, the divisions will take the respective denominations of *first, second, third,* &c., according to position in the column, beginning at the front.

785. The lieutenant colonel, who, at the second command given by the colonel, will have placed himself at a little more than company distance in rear of the right guide of the first division, will assure the right guides on the direction as they successively arrive, by placing himself in their rear.

786. The music will pass to the rear of the column.

787. The battalion being in march, to form the double column at company distance without halting the battalion, the colonel will command:

1. *Double column at half distance.* 2. *Battalion by the right and left flanks.* 3. March (or *double quick*—March).

788. At the first command, each captain will move briskly in front of the centre of his company; the captains of the fourth and fifth will caution their companies to march straight forward; the other captains will caution their companies to face to the right and left.

789. At the command *march*, the fourth and fifth companies will continue to march straight forward; the senior captain will place himself before the centre of his division and command, *Guide right;* the junior captain will place himself in the interval between the two companies. The left guide of the fifth company will place himself on the left of the front rank of the division. The men will take the touch of elbows to the right. The color and general guides will retake their places. The three right companies will face to the left, and the three left companies will face to the right. Each captain will break to the rear two files at the head of his company; the left guides of the right companies, and the right guides of the left companies, will each place himself at the head of the front rank of his company, and the captain by the side of his guide.

790. The third and sixth companies will enter the column and direct themselves parallelly to the first division. Each of the other companies will, in like manner, place itself behind the company of the wing to which it belongs, and will be careful to gain as much ground as possible towards the head of the column.

791. The corresponding companies of each wing will unite into divisions on taking their positions in column, and each captain, the instant the head

of his company arrives at the centre of the column, will command, 1. *Such company by the right (or left) flank.* 2. MARCH. The senior captain of the two companies will place himself in front of the centre of his division, and command, *Guide right;* the junior captain will place himself in the interval between the two companies. The two companies thus formed into a division will take the touch of elbows to the right, and when each division has gained its proper distance, its chief will cause it to march in quick time.

792. When the battalion presents an odd number of companies, the formation will be made in like manner, and the company on either flank which shall find itself without a corresponding one, will place itself at company distance behind the wing to which it belongs.

793. The double column, closed in mass, will be formed according to the same principles and by the same commands, substituting the indication, *closed in mass,* for that of *at half distance.*

794. The double column never being formed when two or more battalions are to be in one general column, it will habitually take the guide to the right, sometimes to the left, or in the centre of the column; in the last case, the command will be, *guide centre.* The column will march and change direction according to the principles prescribed for a simple column by division.

795. The double column at company distance will be closed in mass, or, if in mass, will take half distance, by the commands and means indicated for a simple column by division.

Deployment of the double column, faced to the front.

796. The colonel, wishing to deploy the double column, will place a marker respectively before the right and left files of the first division, and a third before the left file of the right company, same division; which being done, he will cause the two general guides to spring out on the alignment of the markers a little beyond the points at which the respective flanks of the battalion ought to rest; he will then command:

1. *Deploy column.* 2. *Battalion outwards*—FACE
3. MARCH (or *double quick*—MARCH).

797. The column will deploy itself on the two companies at its head, according to the principles prescribed for the deployment of columns in mass. The captains of these companies will each, at the command *march*, place himself on the right of his own company, and align it by the right; the captain of the fourth will then place himself in the rear rank, and the covering sergeant in the rank of file closers, at the moment the captain of the third shall come to its left to align it.

798. The deployment being ended, the colonel will command:

Guides—POSTS.

799 If it be the wish of the colonel to cause the fire to commence pending the deployment, he

will give an order to that effect to the captains of the fourth and fifth companies, and the fire will be executed according to the principles prescribed No. 438.

800. The battalion being in double column and in march, if the colonel shall wish to deploy it without halting the column, he will cause three markers to be posted on the line of battle, and when the head of the column shall arrive near the markers, he will command:

1. *Deploy column.* 2. *Battalion, by the right and left flanks.* 3. March (or *double quick—* March).

801. The column will deploy on the two leading companies, according to the principles prescribed for the deployment of a close column, No. 533 and following; at the command *march*, the chief of the first division will halt it, and the captains of the fourth and fifth companies will align their companies by the right.

802. If the column be in march, and it be the wish of the colonel to deploy the column and to continue to march in the order of battle, he will not cause markers to be established at the head of the column. The movement will be executed by the commands and means indicated No. 800, observing what follows. At the first command, the chief of the first division will command, *Quick time.* At the command *march*, the first division will continue to march in quick time; the colonel will command, *Guide centre.* The captains of the fourth and fifth companies, the color, and the men,

will immediately conform to the principles of the march in line of battle. The companies will take the quick step by the command of their captains, as they successively arrive in line. The movement completed, the colonel may cause the battalion to march in double quick time.

To form the double column into line of battle, faced to the right or left.

803. The double column, being at company distance and at a halt, may be formed into line of battle faced to the right or left; when the colonel shall wish to form it faced to the right, he will command:

1. *Right into line wheel, left companies on the right into line.* 2. *Battalion, guide right.* 3. MARCH (or *double quick*—MARCH).

804. At the first command, each captain will place himself before the centre of his company; the right companies will be cautioned that they will have to wheel to the right into line, the left companies that they will have to march straight forward.

805. At the second command, the left guide of the fourth company will place himself briskly on the direction of the right guides of the column, face to them, and opposite to one of the three last files of his company when in line of battle; the lieutenant colonel will assure him in that position.

806. At the command *march*, briskly repeated by all the captains, the right companies will form

to the right into line of battle, the left companies will put themselves in march in order to form *on* the right into line of battle; these formations will be executed by the means indicated No. 391 and following, No. 416 and following; the lieutenant colonel will assure the guides of the left wing on the line of battle as they successively come upon it.

807. If the column be in march, the colonel will command:

1. *Right into line wheel.* 2. *Left companies, on the right into line.* 3. *Battalion, guide right.* 4. March (or *double quick*—March).

808. At the first command, each captain will place himself promptly before the centre of his company; the right companies will be cautioned that they will have to wheel to the right, and the left companies that they will have to form on the right into line.

809. At the command *march*, briskly repeated, the right companies will form to the right into line, and the left companies on the right into line. These formations will be executed as prescribed Nos. 402, 417, and following.

810. If the colonel should wish to move the battalion forward, at the moment the right companies have completed the wheel, he will command:

5. *Forward.* 6. March (or *double quick—* March).

811. At the command *forward*, the captains of the right companies will command, *Quick time.* At the command *march*, the right companies will cease to wheel and march straight forward. The colonel will then add:

7. *Guide centre.*

812. The movement of the left companies will be executed in double quick time as prescribed above, and as they arrive on the line each captain will cause his company to march in quick time.

813. The column may be formed faced to the left into line of battle according to the same principles.

814. If the column be closed in mass instead of at company distance, these movements will be executed according to the principles prescribed Nos. 417, 502, and 510.

Remark on the deployment of the double column.

815. The depth of the double column, at company distance, being inconsiderable, closing it in mass, if at a halt, in order to deploy it, may be dispensed with; but if it be in march, it will be preferable to cause it so to close, in halting, before deploying.

816. The double column will be deployed habitually on the centre companies, but the colonel may sometimes deploy it on any interior company, or on the first or eighth company.

Article Fourteenth.

Dispositions against Cavalry.

817. A battalion being in column by company, at full distance, right in front, and at a halt, when the colonel shall wish to form it into square, he will first cause divisions to be formed; which being done, he will command:

1. *To form square.* 2. *To half distance, close column.* 3. March (or *double quick*—March).

818. At the command *march*, the column will close to company distance, the second division taking its distance from the rear rank of the first division.

819. At the moment of halting the fourth division, the file closers of each company of which it is composed, passing by the outer flank of their companies will place themselves two paces before the front rank opposite to their respective places in line of battle, and face towards the head of the column.

820. At the commencement of the movement, the major will place himself on the right of the column abreast with the first division; the buglers formed in two ranks will place themselves at platoon distance, behind the inner platoons of the second division.

821. These dispositions being made, the colonel may, according to circumstances, put the column

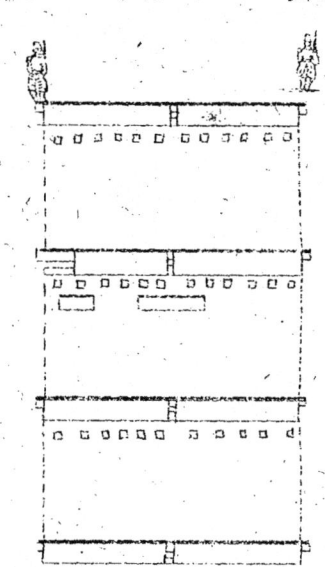

Fig 1.

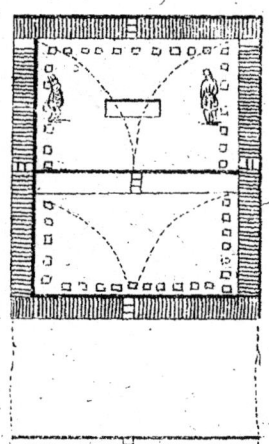

Fig. 2.

SCHOOL OF THE BATTALION—PART V. 183

in march or cause it to form square; if he wish to do the latter, he will command:

1. *Form square.* 2. *Right and left into line, wheel.*

822. At the first command, the lieutenant colonel, facing to the left guides, and the major, facing to those of the right, will align them, from the front, on the respective guides of the fourth division, who will stand fast, holding up their pieces, inverted, perpendicularly; the right guides, in placing themselves on the direction, will take their exact distances.

823. At the second command, the chief of the first division will caution it to stand fast; all the captains of the second and third divisions will place themselves before the centres of their respective companies, and caution them that they will have to wheel, the right companies to the right, and the left companies to the left into line of battle.

824. The color-bearer will step back into the line of file closers, opposite to his place in line of battle, and will be replaced by the corporal of his file, who is in the rear rank; the corporal of the same file who is in the rank of file closers will step into the rear rank.

825. The chief of the fourth division will command: 1. *Fourth division, forward;* 2. *Guide left,* and place himself at the same time two paces outside of its left flank.

826. These dispositions ended, the colonel **will command**:

MARCH (or *double quick*—MARCH).

827. At this command, briskly repeated, the first division will stand fast; but its right file will face to the right, and its left file to the left.

828. The companies of the second and third divisions will wheel to the right and left into line, and the buglers will advance a space equal to the front of a company.

829. The fourth division will close up to form the square, and when it shall have closed, its chief will halt it, face it about, and align it by the rear rank upon the guides of the division, who will, for this purpose, remain faced to the front. The junior captain will pass into the rear rank, now become the front, and the covering sergeant of the left company will place himself behind him in the front rank, become rear. The file closers will, at the same time, close up a pace on the front rank, and the outer file on each flank of the division will face outwards.

830. The square being formed, the colonel will command:

Guides—POSTS.

831. At this command, the chiefs of the first and fourth divisions, as well as the guides, will enter the square.

832. The captains whose companies have formed to the right into line, will remain on the left of

their companies; the left guide of each of those companies will, in the rear rank, cover his captain, and the covering sergeant of each will place himself as a file closer behind the right file of his company.

833. The field and staff will enter the square, the lieutenant colonel placing himself behind the left, and the major behind the right of the first division.

834. If the battalion present ten, instead of eight companies, the fourth division will make the same movements prescribed above for the second and third divisions, and the fifth, the movements prescribed for the fourth division.

835. A battalion ought never to present, near the enemy's cavalry, an odd company. The odd company, under that circumstance, ought, when the battalion is under arms, to be consolidated, for the time, with the other companies.

836. The fronts of the square will be designated as follows: the first division will always be the *first front;* the last division, the *fourth front;* the right companies of the other divisions will form the *second front;* and the left companies of the same divisions the *third front.*

837. A battalion being in column by company, at full distance, right in front, and in march, when the colonel shall wish to form square, he will cause this movement to be executed by the commands and means indicated, No. 817.

838. At the command *march,* the column will close to company distance, as is prescribed, No. 278. When the chief of the fourth division shall command *Quick, march,* the file closers of this

16 *

division will place themselves before the front rank.

839. The major and the buglers will conform to what is prescribed, No. 820.

840. If the colonel shall wish to form square, he will command:

1. *Form square.* 2. *Right and left into line, wheel.* 3. MARCH.

841. At the first command, the chief of the first division will caution it to halt; all the captains of the second and third divisions will rapidly place themselves before the centres of their respective companies, and caution them that they will have to wheel, the right companies to the right, and the left companies to the left into line. The chief of the fourth division will caution it to continue its march, and will hasten to its left flank. At the third command, briskly repeated, the chief of the first division will halt his division and align it to the left, the outer files will face to the right and left, the rest of the movement will be executed as prescribed No. 828 and following.

842. The lieutenant colonel and the major, at the command *march*, will conform to what is prescribed, No. 822.

843. If the battalion, before the square is formed, be in double column, the two leading companies will form the first front, the two rear companies the fourth; the other companies of the right half battalion will form the second, and those of the left half battalion the third front.

844. The first and fourth fronts will be com-

manded by the chiefs of the first and fourth divisions; each of the other two by its senior captain.

845. The commander of each front will place himself four paces behind its present rear rank, and will be replaced momentarily in the command of his company by the next in rank therein.

846. If the column be at full distance, instead of at company distance, as has been supposed, the square will be formed in the manner prescribed, No. 817 or 838, and following; and the dispositions indicated, Nos. 819 and 820, will be executed at the command *form square.*

847. If the column by division, whether double or simple, be in mass, and the colonel shall wish to form it into square, he will first cause it to take company distance; to this effect, he will command:

1. *To form square.* 2. *By the head of column, take half distance.*

848. The divisions will take half distance by the means indicated, No. 324, and following. What is prescribed, No. 820, will be executed as the first and second divisions are put in motion.

849. The colonel will halt the column the moment the third division shall have its distance. As soon as the column is halted, the dispositions indicated, No. 819, will be executed, and when these are completed, the colonel may proceed to form square.

849. If the column be in march, he will also, in the first place, cause company distance to be taken, and, for this purpose, will command:

1. *To form square.* 2. *By the head of column, take half distance.* 3. MARCH (or *double quick—* MARCH).

851. This movement will be executed as prescribed, No. 330, and following. What is prescribed, No. 820, will be executed as the first and second divisions are put in motion.

852. The colonel will proceed to form square the moment the third division shall have its distance; at the command *form square,* the dispositions indicated, No. 819, will be executed. If it be intended merely to *dispose the column for square,* the colonel will not halt the column until the last division has its distance.

853. In a simple column, left in front, these several movements will be executed according to the same principles and by inverse means; but the fronts of the square will have the same designations as if the right of the column were in front, that is, the first division will constitute the first front, and thus of the other subdivisions.

854. The battalion being formed into square, when the colonel shall wish to cause it to advance a distance less than thirty paces, he will command:

1. *By* (such) *front, forward.* 2. MARCH.

855. If it be supposed that the advance be made by the first front, the chief of this front will command:

1. *First division, forward.* 2. *Guide centre.*

856. The chief of the second front will face his front to the left. The captains of the companies composing this front will place themselves outside, and on the right of their left guides, who will replace them in the front rank; the chief of the third front will face his front to the right, and the captains in this front will place themselves outside, and on the left of their covering sergeants; the chief of the fourth front will face his front about, and command: 1. *Fourth division, forward;* 2. *Guide centre.* The captain who is in the centre of the first front, will be charged with the direction of the march, and will regulate himself by the means indicated in the school of the company, No. 89.

857. At the command *march*, the square will put itself in motion; the companies marching by the flank will be careful not to lose their distances. The chief of the fourth division will cause his division to keep constantly closed on the flanks of the second and third fronts.

857. This movement will only be executed in quick time.

858. The lieutenant colonel will place himself in rear of the file of direction in order to regulate his march.

860. If the colonel should wish to halt the square, he will command:

> 1. *Battalion.* 2. **Halt.**

861. At the second command, the square will halt; the fourth front will face about immediately, and without further command; the second and third fronts will face outwards; the captains of companies will resume their places as in square.

862. In moving the square forward by the second, third, or fourth fronts, the same rules will be observed.

863. The battalion being formed into square, when the colonel shall wish to cause it to advance a greater distance than thirty paces, he will command:

> 1. *Form column.*

864. The chief of the first front will command:

> 1. *First division forward.* 2. *Guide left.*

865. The commander of the fourth front will caution it to stand fast; the commander of the second front will cause it to face to the left, and then command, *By company, by file left.* The commander of the third front will cause it to face to the right, and then command, *By company, by file right.* At the moment the second and third fronts face to the left and right, each captain will cause to break to the rear the two leading files of his company.

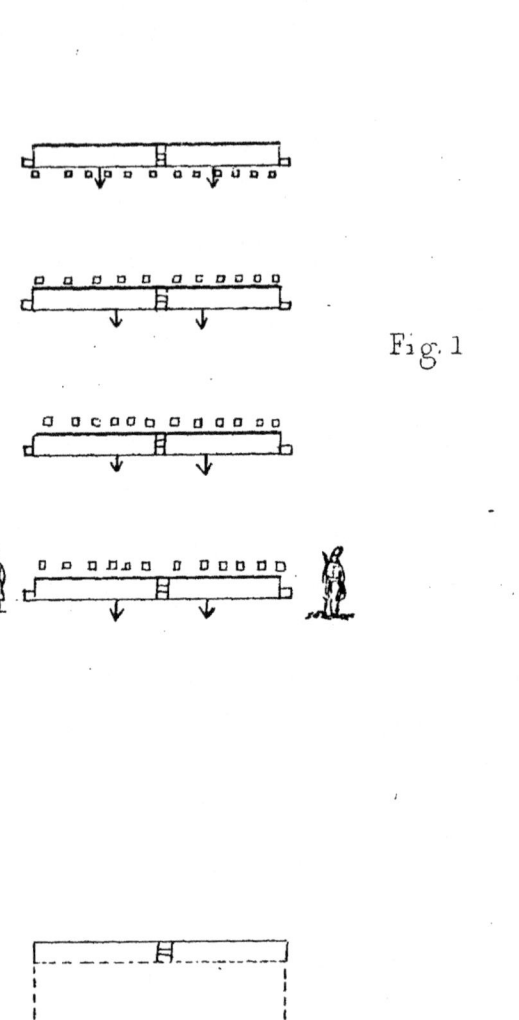

Fig. 1

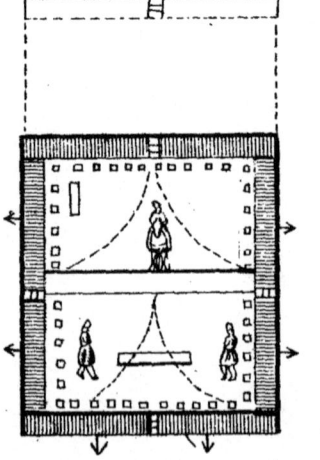

Fig. 2

866. These dispositions being made, the colonel will command:

3. MARCH (or *double quick*—MARCH).

867. At this command, the first front will march forward; its chief will halt it when it shall have advanced a space equal to half its front, and align it by the left.

868. The corresponding companies of the second and third fronts will wheel by file to the left and right, and march to meet each other behind the centre of the first division, and the moment they unite, the captain of each company will halt his company and face it to the front. The division being re-formed, its chief will align it by the left.

869. The commander of the fourth front will cause it to face about: its file closers will remain before the front rank.

870. The column being thus re-formed, the colonel may put it in march by the commands and means prescribed, No. 164, and following; the right guides will preserve company distance exactly as the directing guides.

871. When the colonel shall wish to re-form square, he will give the commands indicated, No. 840.

872. To cause the square to march in retreat a distance greater than thirty paces, the colonel will first cause column to be formed as indicated No. 863; and when formed, he will cause it to face by the rear rank; to this end, he will command:

1. *To march in retreat.* 2. *Face by the rear rank.* 3. *Battalion about*—FACE.

873. At the second command, the file closers of the interior divisions will place themselves, passing by the outer flanks of their respective companies, behind the front rank opposite to their places in line of battle; the file closers of the other divisions will stand fast.

874. At the third command, the battalion will face about; each chief of division will place himself before its rear rank, become front, passing through the interval between its two companies; the guides will step into the rear rank, now front.

875. The column being thus disposed, the colonel may put it in march, or cause it to form square as if it were faced by the front rank. The square being formed, its fronts will preserve the same designations they had when faced by the front rank.

876. The battalion being in square by the rear rank, when the colonel shall wish to march it in retreat or in advance, a distance less than thirty paces, he will conform to what is prescribed No. 854 and following; otherwise, he will re-form the column according to the principles prescribed No. 863 by marching forward the fourth front.

877. If the square is to be marched to the front a distance greater than thirty paces, the colonel will face the column by the front rank; to this end, he will command:

1. *To march in advance.* 2. *Face by the front rank.* 3. *Battalion about*—FACE.

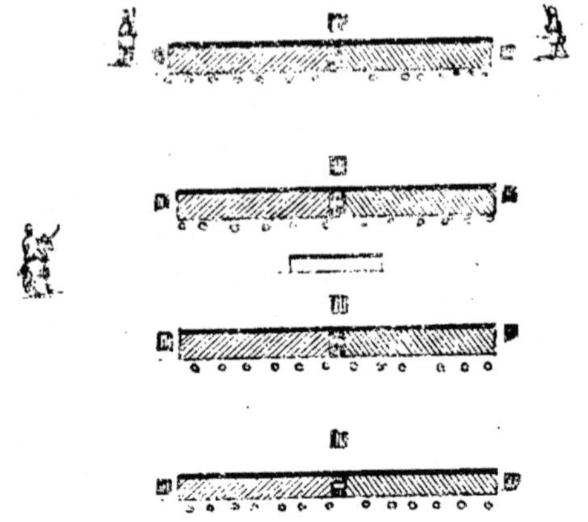

Fig. 1

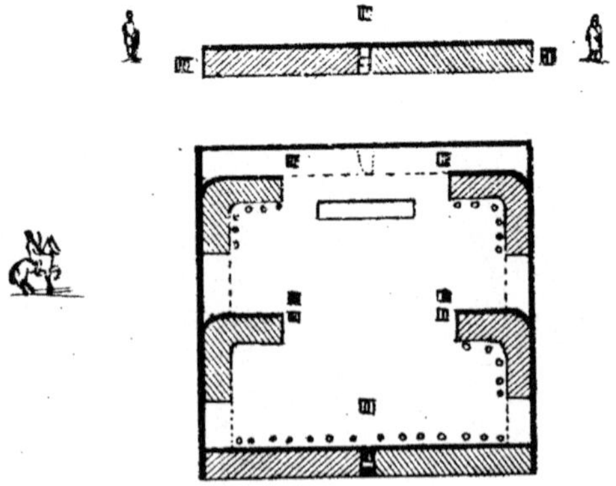

Fig. 2

878. Which will be executed as prescribed No. 873 and following.

879. If the column be marching in advance, and the colonel shall wish to march it in retreat, he will command:

1. *To march in retreat.* 2. *Battalion right about.* 3. MARCH (or *double quick*—MARCH).

880. At the second command, the file closers of the second and third divisions will place themselves rapidly before the front rank of their respective divisions. At the command *march*, the column will face about and move off to the rear; the chiefs of divisions and the guides will conform to what is prescribed No. 874.

881. If the column be marching in retreat, and the colonel shall wish to march it in advance, he will command:

1. *To march in advance.* 2. *Battalion right about.* 3. MARCH (or *double quick*—MARCH).

882. At the second command, the file closers of the second and third divisions will place themselves before the rear rank of their respective divisions; at the third, the column will face by the front rank.

To reduce the square.

883. The colonel, wishing to break the square, will command:

1. *Reduce square.* 2. MARCH (or *double quick*—MARCH).

884. This movement will be executed in the manner indicated, No. 863 and following; but the file closers of the fourth front will place themselves behind the rear rank the moment it faces about; the field and staff, the color-bearer and buglers, will, at the same time, return to their places in column.

To form square from line of battle.

885. A battalion deployed, may be formed into square in a direction either parallel or perpendicular to the line of battle.

886. In the first case, the colonel will cause the battalion to break by division to the rear, by the right or left, and then close the column to half distance, as indicated, No. 817, and following.

887. In the second case, he will ploy the battalion into simple column by division at half distance in rear of the right or left division, or into column doubled on the centre.

888. To ploy the battalion into column upon one of the flank divisions, the colonel will command:

1. *To form square.* 2. *Column at half distance by division.* 3. *On the first* (or *fourth*) *division.* 4. *Battalion right* (or *left*)—Face. 5. March (or *double quick*—March).

889. This movement will be executed according to the principles prescribed No. 119 and following.

890. If the battalion be marching in line of battle, and the colonel shall wish to form square

in a direction perpendicular to the line of battle, he will command:

1. *To form square.* 2. *On the first (or fourth) division, form column.* 3. *Battalion by the right (or left) flank.* 4. March (or *double quick*—March).

891. This movement will be executed according to the principles prescribed for ploying a column by division at half distance, No. 150. The chief of the first division will halt his division at the command *march.*

892. To ploy the battalion into double column, the colonel will command:

1. *To form square.* 2. *Double column at half distance* 3. *Battalion inwards*—Face. 4. March (or *double quick*—March).

893. This movement will be executed as prescribed No. 778 and following.

894. The battalion being in march, to ploy it into double column to form square, the colonel will command:

1. *To form square.* 2. *Form double column.* 3. *Battalion by the right and left flanks.* 4. March (or *double quick*—March).

895. This movement will be executed as prescribed No. 788. The chief of the leading division will halt his division at the command *march.*

Observations relative to the formation of squares in two ranks.

896. When the colonel shall judge it proper to have a reserve, this reserve, in a column of three divisions, will be formed of the inner platoons of the second division. The second division will, in this case, close to platoon distance on the first division. When the square is formed, the reserve platoons will move forward a distance nearly equal to a platoon front.

897. In re-forming column, the first division will move forward platoon, instead of company distance.

898. If the column be formed of four divisions, the inner platoons of the third division will compose the reserve; then, in re-forming column, the first division will conform to the general rule, and the chief of the third, as soon as his division is formed, will close it to platoon distance on the second division. The colonel may, if necessary, form the reserve of the entire third division. In this case, the movement will be executed in the following manner.

899. If the column be at full distance, when it shall close, at the command *to form square,* to half distance, the chief of the third division will cause four files to break to the rear from the right and left of his division; the guides will close upon the outer files remaining in line, and the left guide will march exactly in the trace of the file immediately in front of him. This division will then close in mass on the second division; and the chief

SCHOOL OF THE BATTALION—PART V. 197

of the fourth division will close to half distance on the same division.

900. At the command *form square*, the chief of the reserve division will command, 1. *Third division forward.* 2. *Guide centre;* at this command, the guides on the flanks will fall into the line of file closers. At the command *march*, the reserve will move forward the distance of a company front. When halted, its chief will cause the platoons to be doubled, and for this purpose will command:

1. *On the centre double platoons.* 2. MARCH.

901. At the first command, the chiefs of platoon will place themselves in front of the centre of their respective platoons; the chief of each outer platoon will face his platoon towards the centre, and cause to break to the rear two files from the left or right. At the command *march*, the outer platoons will direct their march so as to double on the centre platoon at the distance of four paces; their chiefs will align these outer platoons on the centre, and the files previously broken to the rear will come into line.

902. If the column be at half, instead of full distance, the colonel before forming square will order the chiefs of the third and fourth divisions to move forward their divisions as prescribed No. 899.

903. If the column be closed in mass, at the command *to form square*, the chief of the third division will break four files to the rear from each of the flanks as prescribed No. 899.

904. The colonel will halt the column as soon

17 *

as the second division shall have gained its distance.

905. If the colonel shall wish the column to continue marching, at the command, *by the head of column take half distance,* the chief of the re serve division will give his cautionary commands in sufficient time to place his division in motion simultaneously with the one which precedes it. The chief of the fourth division will give the command *march* at the instant there is company distance between his division and the second.

906. When the colonel shall wish to re-form the column, at the command *form column,* the chief of the third division will command, *Form division;* at this command, the chiefs of the outer platoons which have doubled in rear of the centre platoons, will give the commands and make the preparatory movements for deploying on the centre platoons, which will be executed at the command *march* given by the colonel and briskly repeated by the chief of this division. The division being re-formed, the chiefs of the outer platoons will retake their places in column, and the chief of this division will again cause four files from each of its flanks to break to the rear.

907. If before the formation of the square, the column had been left in front, it would be formed by the same commands and according to the same principles. The second division, in this case, would form the reserve.

908. The column being formed, if the colonel should wish to march it in retreat he will face it by the rear rank. The files of the third division broken off to the rear, will face about with the

battalion, and when the column is put in motion will march in front of the rear rank. But should the colonel wish to re-form the square, he will cause the battalion to face by the front rank.

909. If the battalion be in line, instead of in column, the chief of the reserve division will bring it into column in such manner that there may be a distance of only four paces between this division and the one which is to be immediately in front of it; and when this division is halted and aligned, its chief will cause the usual number of files to be broken to the rear. The chief of the division which should occupy in column a position immediately in rear of the reserve division will, on entering the column, take a distance of twelve paces between it and the division established immediately in front of the reserve division.

Squares in four ranks.

910. If the square formed in two ranks, according to the preceding rules, should not be deemed sufficiently strong, the colonel may cause the square to be formed in four ranks.

911. The battalion being in column by company at full distance, right in front, and at a halt, when the colonel shall wish to form square in four ranks, he will first cause divisions to be formed, which being executed, he will command:

1. *To form square in four ranks.* 2. *To half distance. close column.* 3. MARCH (or *double quick— MARCH*).

912. At the first command, the chief of the first division will caution the right company to face to the left, and the left company to face to the right. The chiefs of the other divisions will caution their divisions to move forward.

913. At the command *march*, the right company of the first division will form into four ranks on its left file, and the left company into four ranks on its right file. The formation ended, the chief of this division will align it by the left.

914. The other divisions will move forward and double their files marching; the right company of each division will double on its left file, and the left company on its right file. The formation completed, each chief of division will command, *Guide left*. Each chief will halt his division when it shall have the distance of a company front in four ranks from the preceding one, counting from its rear rank, and will align his division by the left. At the instant the fourth division is halted, the file closers will move rapidly before its front rank.

915. The colonel will form square, re-form column, and reduce square in four ranks, by the same commands and means as prescribed for a battalion in two ranks.

916. If the square formed in four ranks be reduced and at a halt, and the colonel shall wish to form the battalion into two ranks, he will command:

1. *In two ranks undouble files.* 2. *Battalion outwards*—Face. 3. March.

917. At the first command, the captains will step before the centres of their respective compa-

nies, and those on the right will caution them to face to the right, and those on the left to face to the left.

918. At the second command, the battalion will face to the right and left.

919. At the command *march*, each company will undouble its files and re-form into two ranks as indicated in the school of the company No. 376 and following. Each captain will halt his company and face it to the front. The formation completed, each chief of division will align his division by the left.

920. If the column be in march, with divisions formed in four ranks, and the colonel shall wish to re-form them into two ranks, he will command:

1. *Guide centre.* 2. *In two ranks, undouble files.* 3. March.

921. The captain, placed in the centre of each division, will continue to march straight to the front, as will also the left file of the right company, and the right file of the left company. Each company will then be re-formed into two ranks, as prescribed in the school of the company.

922. The battalion being formed into two ranks, the colonel will command, *Guide left* (or *right*).

923. To form square in four ranks on one of the flank divisions, the colonel will command:

1. *To form square, in four ranks.* 2. *Column at half distance, by division.* 3. *On the first* (or *fourth*) *division.* 4. *Battalion, right* (or *left*)— Face. 5. March (or *double quick*—March).

924. At the second command, each chief of division will place himself before the centre of his division, and caution it to face to the right.

925. At the fourth command, the right guide of the first division will remain faced to the front, the battalion will face to the right.

926. At the command *march*, the first file of four men of the first division will face to the front remaining doubled. All the other files of four men will step off together, and each in succession will close up to its proper distance on the file preceding it, and face to the front, remaining doubled. When the last file shall have closed, the chief of division will command, *Left*—Dress.

927. The other divisions will ploy into column in the same manner as with a battalion in two ranks, observing what follows: the chiefs of division, instead of allowing their divisions to file past them on entering the column, will continue to lead them, and as each division shall arrive on a line with the right guide of the first division, its chief will halt the right guide, who will immediately face to the front; the first file of four men will also halt at the same time and face to the front, remaining doubled. The second file will close on the first, and when closed, halt, and face to the front, remaining doubled. All the other files will execute successively what has just been prescribed for the second. When the last file shall have closed, the chief of division will command, *Left*—Dress.

SCHOOL OF THE BATTALION—PART V. 203

928. If the battalion be in march, the colonel will command:

1. *To form square, in four ranks.* 2. *On the first division, form column.* 3. *Battalion, by the right flank.* 4. MARCH (or *double quick—* MARCH).

929. At the second command, each chief of division will step in front of the centre of his division and caution it to face by the right flank. The chief of the first division will caution his covering sergeant to halt, and remain faced to the front.

930. At the command *march*, the battalion will face to the right; the covering sergeant of the first division will halt and remain faced to the front, the first division will then form into four ranks as heretofore prescribed. The other divisions will ploy into column in the same manner as if the movement had taken place from a halt.

931. If the colonel should wish to form a perpendicular square in four ranks, by double column, he will command:

1. *To form square, in four ranks.* 2. *Double column, at half distance.* 3. *Battalion inwards* —FACE. 4. MARCH (or *double quick*—MARCH).

932. At the second command, the captains of companies will place themselves before the centres of their respective companies, and caution those on the right to face to the left, and those on the left to face to the right. The captain of the fifth

company will caution his covering sergeant to stand fast.

933. At the third command, the battalion will face to the left and right; at the command *march*, the left file of the fourth, and the right file of the fifth company, will face to the front, remaining doubled. The fourth company will close successively by file of fours on the left file, and the fifth company, in like manner, on the right file; the files will face to the front, remaining doubled. The formation completed, the chief of division will command, *Right dress.* The junior captain will place himself in the interval between the two companies.

934. The other companies will close as prescribed for the double column in two ranks, observing what follows: each captain will halt the leading guide of his company the moment the head of his company arrives on a line with the centre of the column. In the right companies, the left guides will step into the line of file closers, and the left file of four men will face immediately to the front, remaining doubled, and by the side of the right guide of the left company. The companies will each form into four ranks, as prescribed No. 926, the right companies on the left file, and the left companies on the right file. The formation completed, the junior captain will place himself between the two companies, and the senior will command, *Right dress.*

935. If the battalion be in march, the colonel will command:

205

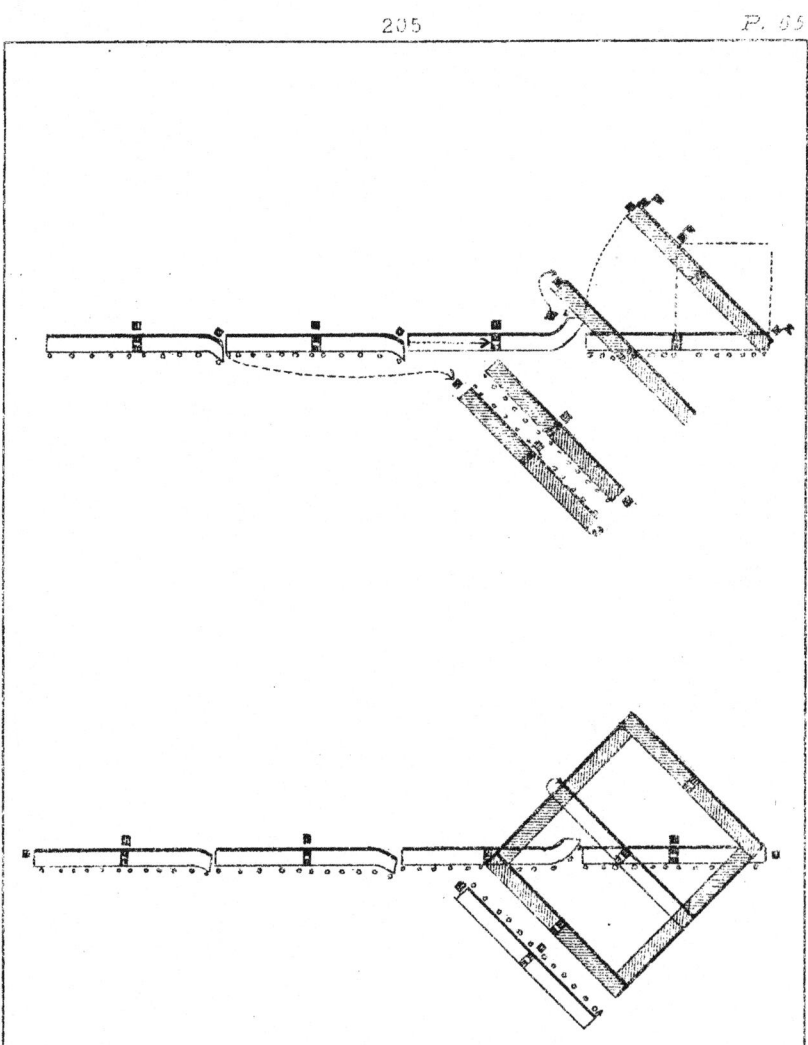

SCHOOL OF THE BATTALION—PART V. 205

1. *To form square, in four ranks.* 2. *Form double column.* 2. *Battalion by the right and left flanks.* 4. MARCH (or *double quick*—MARCH).

936. At the second command, the captains will place themselves before the centres of their respective companies, and those on the right will caution them to face by the left flank, and those on the left to face by the right flank; the captain of the fifth company will caution his covering sergeant to halt, and remain faced to the front.

937. At the command *march*, the fourth and fifth companies will halt. The battalion will face to the left and right; the covering sergeant of the fifth company will halt and remain faced to the front, the movement will then be executed as if the battalion was at a halt.

Oblique squares.

938. The battalion being in line of battle, when the colonel shall wish to form the oblique square, he will command:

1. *To form oblique square.* 2. *On the first division form column.*

939. At the second command, the lieutenant colonel will trace the alignment of the first division in the following manner: he will place himself before and near the right file of this division, face to the left, march twelve paces along the front rank, halt, face to the right, march twelve paces

perpendicularly to the front, halt again, face to the right, and immediately place a marker at this point. The covering sergeant of the right company will step, at the same time, before its right file, face to the left, and conform the line of his shoulders to that of the shoulders of the marker established by the lieutenant colonel. These two markers being established, the lieutenant colonel will place a third marker on the same alignment, at the point where the left of the division will halt.

940. The chiefs of division will place themselves in front of the centres of their divisions; the chief of the first division will immediately establish it by a wheel to the right on a fixed pivot, against the markers, and align it by the left. The chiefs of the other divisions will caution them to face to the right. The colonel will then command:

3. *Battalion right*—FACE. 4. MARCH (or *double quick*—MARCH).

941. The three rear divisions will direct their march so as to place themselves at half distance from each other, and in the rear of the first division, as previously indicated, observing what follows:

942. The chief of the second division, instead of breaking the headmost files to the rear, will break them to the front, and at the command *march*, will conduct his division towards the point of entrance into the column. Arrived at this point, he will halt in his own person, cause

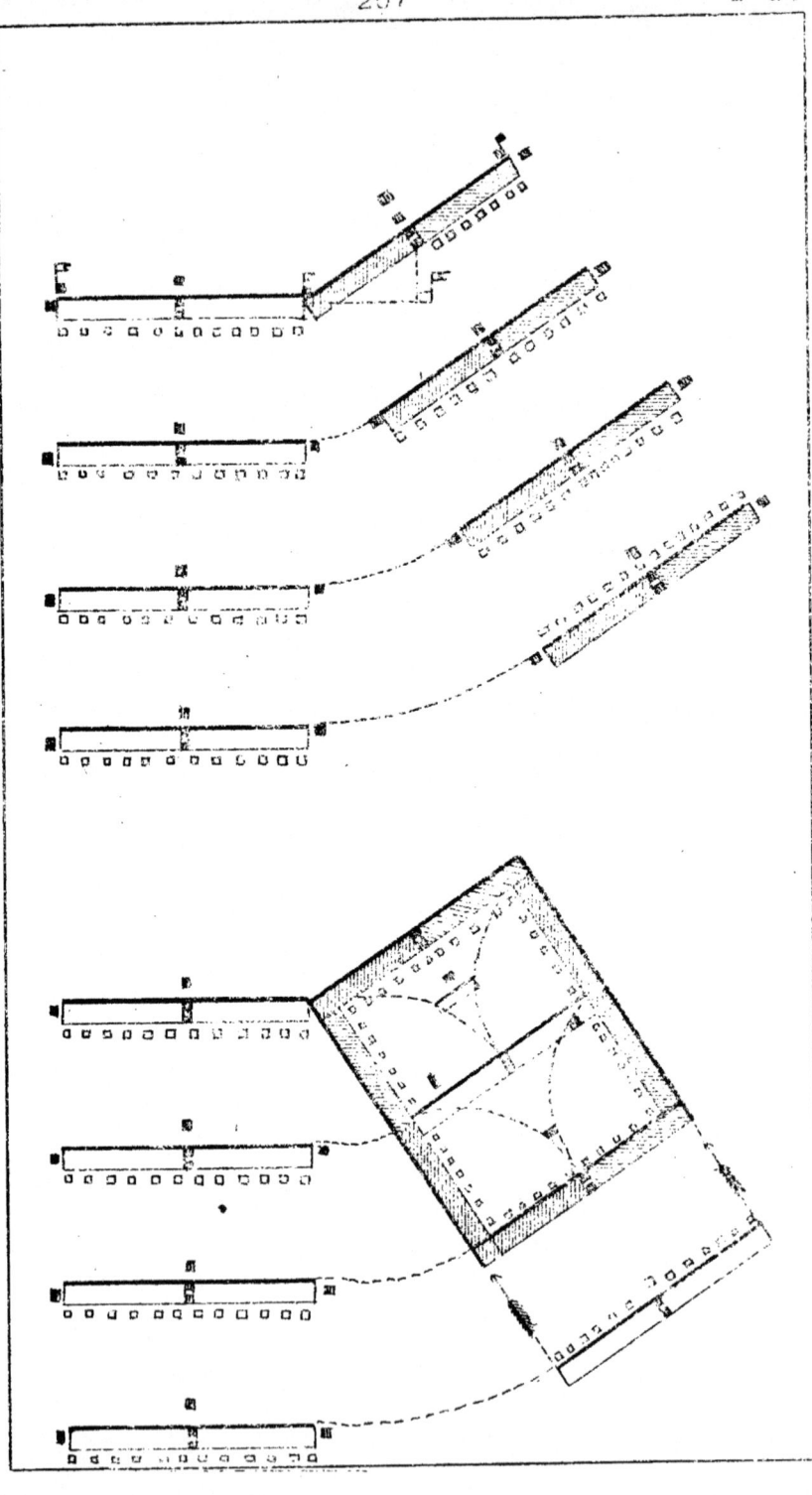

SCHOOL OF THE BATTALION—PART V. 207

his division to wheel by file to the right, instructing the right guide to direct himself parallelly to the first division; and as soon as the left file has passed, its chief will halt the division, and align it by the left. The other divisions will break to the rear, but slightly; each will enter the column as prescribed for the second, and the moment the battalion is ployed into column, the colonel will cause it to form square.

943. The formation of a battalion into oblique square on the left division, will be executed according to the same principles and by inverse means.

944. Should the battalion be in march, the colonel will first cause it to halt.

945. In the preceding example, the battalion was supposed to be deployed; but if it be already formed in column, the desired obliquity will be established by causing it to change direction by the flank; to this end, the colonel will command:

1. *To form oblique square.* 2. *Change direction by the right* (or *left*) *flank.*

946. At the second command, the lieutenant colonel will trace the new direction in the following manner; he will place before the right and left files of the headmost division, two markers, and a third on the prolongation of the first two, on the side of the change of direction, and at twelve paces from the flank of the column. He will then place himself before the third marker, march twelve paces perpendicularly to the front,

halt, and finish tracing the new direction in the manner indicated, No. 939.

947. The colonel will then command:

3. *Battalion right* (or *left*)—Face. 4. March (or *double quick*—March).

948. The change of direction having been executed, the colonel will cause the square to be formed.

949. Should the column be in march, the colonel will first cause it to halt.

950. Oblique squares in four ranks, will be executed by the same means, and according to the principles prescribed for the formation of squares in four ranks.

951. Whether the battalion be ployed into simple or double column, the particular dispositions for the formation of the square will be executed as prescribed No. 819 and following. The division which is to form the rear of the column, will be closed in mass, and as soon as it is aligned, the major will rectify the position of the guides on the side of the column opposite to the direction.

952. If it be the wish of the colonel merely to prepare for square, he will in all formations with that view substitute the command *prepare for square* in place of *to form square*, and in that case, the last division will enter the column at company distance.

Remarks on the formation of squares.

953. It is a general principle that a column by

company, which is to be formed into square, will first form divisions, and close to half distance. Nevertheless, if it find itself suddenly threatened by cavalry without sufficient time to form divisions, the colonel will cause the column to close to platoon distance and then form square by the commands and means which have been indicated; the leading and rearmost companies will conform themselves to what has been prescribed for divisions in those positions. The other companies will form by platoon to the right and left into line of battle, and each chief of platoon, after having halted it, will place himself on the line, as if the platoon were a company, and he will be covered by the guide in the rear rank.

954. A battalion in column at full distance, having to form square, will always close on the leading subdivision; and a column closed in mass, will always, for the same purpose, take distances by the head. In either case, the second subdivision should be careful, in taking its distance, to reckon from the rear rank of the subdivision in front of it.

955. If a column by company should be required to form square in four ranks, the doubling of files will always take place on the file next the guide.

956. When a column, disposed to form square, shall be in march, it will change direction as a column at half distance; thus, having to execute this movement, the column will take the guide on the side opposite to that to which the change of direction is to be made, if *that* be not already the side of the guide.

957. A column doubled on the centre at company

distance or closed in mass, may be formed into square according to the same principles as a simple column.

958. When a battalion is ployed, with a view to the square, it will always be in rear of the right or left division, in order that it may be able to commence firing, pending the execution of the movement. The double column, also, affords this advantage, and being more promptly formed than any other, it will habitually be employed, unless particular circumstances cause a different formation to be preferred.

959. A battalion, in square, will never use any other than the fire by file and by rank; the color being in the line of file closers, its guard will not fall back as prescribed No. 41; it will fire like the men of the company of which it forms a part.

960. If the square be formed in four ranks, the first two ranks will alone execute the firings prescribed above; the other two ranks will remain either at shoulder or support arms.

961. The formation of the square being often necessary in war, and being the most complicated of the manœuvres, it will be as frequently repeated as the supposed necessity may require, in order to render its mechanism familiar to both officers and men.

962. In the execution of this manœuvre, the colonel will carefully observe that the divers movements which it involves succeed each other without loss of time, but also without confusion; for, if the rapidity of cavalry movements requires the greatest promptitude in the formation of squares, so, on the other hand, precipitancy always results

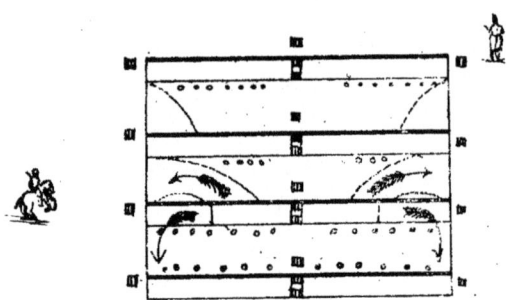

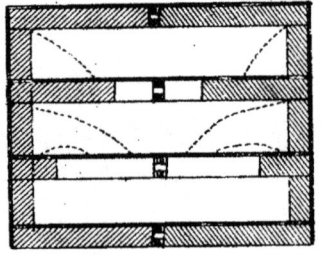

in disorder, and in no circumstance is disorder more to be avoided.

963. When the colonel shall wish to cover by skirmishers the movements of a column preparing to form square, he will detach for this purpose one or two inner platoons of one of the interior divisions of the column. In this case, the exterior platoons of this division and the following subdivisions, will, according to circumstances, close on the preceding subdivision, in such manner, that there may be between them only the distance necessary for forming into line.

964. When the colonel shall be ready to form square, he will, in order to recall the skirmishers, cause *to the color* to be sounded. If on the return of the skirmishers, there be not room for them to form into line of battle, they will double on the outer platoons of their respective companies.

Column against cavalry.

965. When a column closed in mass has to form square, it will begin by taking company distance; but if so suddenly threatened by cavalry as not to allow time for this disposition, it will be formed in the following manner:

966. The colonel will command:

1. *Column against cavalry.* 2. March.

967. At the first command, the chief of the leading division will caution it to stand fast and pass behind the rear rank; in the interior divisions each captain will promptly designate the number

of files necessary to close the interval between his company and the one in front of it. The captains of the divisions next to the one in rear, in addition to closing the interval in front, will also close up the interval which separates this division from the last; the chief of the fourth division will caution it to face about, and its file closers will pass briskly before the front rank.

968. At the command *march*, the guides of each division will place themselves rapidly in the line of file closers. The first division will stand fast, the fourth will face about, the outer file of each of these divisions will then face outwards; in the other divisions the files designated for closing the intervals will form to the right and left into line, but in the division next to the rearmost one, the first files that come into line will close to the right or left until they join the rear division. The files of each company which remain in column will close on their outer files, formed into line, in order to create a vacant space in the middle of the column.

969. If the column be in march, the *column against cavalry* will be formed by the same commands and means. At the command *march*, the first and fourth divisions will halt and the latter division will face about; the interior divisions will conform to what has been prescribed above.

970. The battalion being no longer threatened by cavalry, the colonel will command:

1. *Form column.* 2. March.

971. At the command *march*, the files in column will close to the left and right to make room for

those in line who will retake their places in column by stepping backwards, except those closing the interval between the two rear divisions, who will take their places in column by a flank movement. The fourth division will face about, the guides will resume their places.

972. If the colonel should be so pressed as not to have time to order bayonets to be fixed, the men will fix them, without command or signal, at the cautionary command, *column against cavalry*.

973. As this manœuvre is often used in war, and with decided advantage, the colonel will frequently cause it to be executed in order to render it familiar.

Article Fifteenth.

The rally.

974. The battalion being in line of battle, the colonel will sometimes cause the disperse to be sounded, at which signal, the battalion will break and disperse.

975. When the colonel shall wish to rally the battalion, he will cause *to the color* to be sounded, and at the same time place two markers and the color-bearer in the direction he may wish to give the battalion.

976. Each captain will rally his company about six paces in rear of the place it is to occupy in line of battle.

977. The colonel will cause the color-company to be promptly established against the markers,

and each company by the command of its captain will be aligned on the color-company according to the principles heretofore prescribed.

978. When the colonel shall wish to rally the battalion in column, he will cause *the assembly* to be sounded, and place two markers before the position to be occupied by the first company; the captain of this company will rally his company in rear of the two markers, and each of the other captains will rally his company at platoon distance, behind the one which should precede it in the order in column.

Article Sixteenth.

Rules for manœuvring by the rear rank.

979. It may often be necessary to cause a battalion to manœuvre by the rear rank; when the case presents itself, the following rules will be observed.

980. The battalion being by the front rank, when the colonel shall wish to manœuvre by the rear rank, he will command:

1. *Face by the rear rank.* 2. *Battalion.*
3. *About*—Face.

981. If the battalion be deployed, this movement will be executed as has been indicated for the fire by the rear rank.

982. If the battalion be in column by company, or by platoon, right or left in front, the chiefs of subdivision, to take their new places in column,

SCHOOL OF THE BATTALION—PART V. 215

will each pass by the left flank of his subdivision, and the file closers by the right flank; the guides will place themselves in the rear rank.

983. If the column be formed by division, the chiefs of division will each pass by the interval in the centre of his division, and the file closers by the outer flanks of their respective companies; the junior captain in each division will step into the rear rank, and be covered in the front rank by the covering sergeant of the left company.

984. The lieutenant colonel will place himself abreast with the leading subdivision, and the major abreast with the rearmost one.

985. The battalion being faced by the rear rank, companies, divisions, and wings, will preserve their prior denominations respectively.

986. The manœuvres by the rear rank will be executed by the same commands and on the same principles as if the battalion faced by the front rank; but in such manner that when the battalion shall be brought to its proper front, all the subdivisions may find themselves in their regular order from right to left.

987. According to this principle, when a column faced by the rear rank is deployed, the subdivisions which, in line of battle by the front rank, ought to find themselves on the right of the subdivision on which the deployment is made, will face to the left; and those which ought to be placed on its left, will face to the right.

988. When a battalion in line of battle, faced by the rear rank, is to be ployed into column, the colonel will announce, in the commands, *left* or *right in front*, according as it may be intended

that the first or last subdivision shall be at the head of the column, because the first subdivision is on the left, and the last on the right of the battalion faced by the rear rank. The column by the rear rank will take the guide to the right, if the first subdivision be in front, and to the left in the reverse case.

989. A column, faced by the rear rank, will be brought to its proper front by the means heretofore prescribed. If the column be formed by company, or by platoon, the chiefs of subdivision, in order to take their new places in column, will pass by the left of subdivisions, now right, and the file closers by the right, now left.

SCHOOL OF THE BATTALION,

ARRANGED INTO LESSONS.

LESSON FIRST.

ARTICLE I.—Open ranks (No. 23).
ARTICLE II.—Close ranks (No. 29).
ARTICLE III.—Manual of arms (No. 30). Loading at will (No. 31).
ARTICLE IV.—Different fires by the front rank (No. 39), and by the rear rank (No. 54).

LESSON SECOND.

ARTICLE I.—Break by company to the right (No. 69), or to the left (No. 74).
ARTICLE II.—March in column, at the cadenced step, a considerable distance (No. 164). Change of direction (No. 231). Diminish and increase front in marching (No. 196). March in retreat (No. 170).

Article III.—Halt the column (No. 239). Form it to the left or right into line of battle (No. 390). Execute this formation, the column marching (No. 402).

Article IV.—Execute the countermarch, and repeat the same movements (No. 351).

Article V.—Form column into line of battle, **to the right or left, by inversion** (No. 407).

Lesson Third.

Article I.—Break by company to the **rear by the right or left**, the battalion being at a halt (No. 87), or marching (No. 94).

Article II.—March in the route step (No. 198). Cause to be executed, at this gait and in double quick time, the divers movements incident to the column in route, and cause the cadenced step to be resumed.

Article III.—Form the column forward into line of battle (Nos. 440, 452), faced to the rear into line of battle (Nos. 466, 480), the battalion being at a halt, or marching. Form the column forward into line, and continue the march in this order (No. 456).

Article IV.—Form the column on the right (No. 416), or the left (No. 432), into line of battle.

Article V.—March by the flank (No. 722), and form companies into line, marching.

Article VI.—The column supposed to arrive before (No. 175) or behind the line of battle (No. 184), to prolong it on that line.

SCHOOL OF THE BATTALION. 219

Article VII.—Change front forward (No. 743), or in rear (No. 760), on the right or left of companies, in directions perpendicular or oblique.

Article VIII.—March by the right flank (No. 722), or by the left flank (No. 725). Change direction by file (No. 730). Form the battalion into line of battle, on the right or left, by file (No. 735).

Article IX.—Pass the defile in retreat by the right (No. 709), or by the left flank (No. 720).

Lesson Fourth.

Article I.—Break by division to the rear, by the right or left, the battalion being at a halt or marching (No. 102).

Article II.—March in column by division (No. 161). Diminish and increase front by company (No. 196).

Article III.—Close the column to half distance on the headmost or the rearmost division (No. 278).

Article IV.—March in column at half distance (No. 281), and change direction (No. 287).

Article V.—The column being at half distance, to form square at a halt (No. 817), or marching (No. 837).

Article VI.—The battalion being in square, to march to the front (No. 854). Halt the square (No. 860). Form column to march to the front (No. 863), or in retreat (No. 872). Re-form the square (No. 875).

Article VII.—Reduce the square (No. 883).

Article VIII.—Close the column in mass or the headmost or rearmost division (No. 279).

Article IX.—March in column closed in mass, and change direction by the front of subdivisions (No. 288).

Article X.—Form the column against cavalry (No. 966).

Article XI.—Take distances by the head (Nos. 323 and 330), or on rear of the column (No. 333), the column being at a halt or marching.

Article XII.—The column being by company, cause to be executed the movements indicated in Nos. 3, 4, 5, 6, 7, 8, 9, 10 and 11 of this lesson. The column being at half distance, or closed in mass, to form to the left, or right, into line, wheel, on the rear of the column (No. 502).

Article XIII.—The column being by company, form divisions from a halt (No. 364), or in march (No. 376).

Article XIV.—The column being by division, to form it to the left or right into line of battle at a halt (No. 401), or in march (No. 402).

Lesson Fifth.

Article I.—The battalion being in line of battle, and at a halt, to ploy it by division into column closed in mass on the right division (No. 119), or on the left division (No. 141), or on an interior division (No. 143), the right or left in front. Ploy the battalion marching in line of battle on the right or left division (No. 149).

ARTICLE II.—Execute the countermarch (No. 352).

ARTICLE III.—Change direction to the right (No. 307), to the left (No. 313), by the flank of the column.

ARTICLE IV.—Deploy the column on the right division (No. 514), on the left division (No. 541), or on any interior division, the column being at a halt, or marching (No. 563).

ARTICLE V.—Ploy the battalion into column by division at half distance, marching (No. 556).

ARTICLE VI.—Ploy the battalion by company, closed in mass, and form it on the right or left into line of battle (No. 577).

ARTICLE VII.—Ploy the battalion into double column, at half distance (No. 777), or closed in mass (No. 793), the battalion being at a halt, or marching.

ARTICLE VIII.—March in this order, and change direction (No. 794).

ARTICLE IX.—Deploy the column at a halt (No. 796), or marching (No. 800), and without suspending the march (No. 802).

ARTICLE X.—The double column being at half distance, form it into line of battle faced to the right or left (No. 803), the column being in march (No. 807). Execute the same movement without suspending the march (No. 810).

ARTICLE XI.—Perpendicular or parallel squares, the battalion being deployed (Nos. 889, 895). Oblique squares, the battalion being in line of battle (No. 938), or in column (No. 945). Squares in four ranks (No. 911).

Lesson Sixth.

Article I.—March in line of battle (No. 587). Halt the battalion (No. 635), and align it (No. 640).

Article II.—Change direction in line of battle, advancing (No. 652), or in retreat (No. 681). Execute passage of obstacles (No. 682).

Article III.—Oblique march in line of battle (No. 623).

Article IV.—Disperse and rally the battalion in line of battle (No. 974), and rally the battalion in column by company (No. 978).

REMARKS

ON THE SCHOOL OF THE BATTALION.

In every course of instruction, the first lesson will be executed several times in the order in which it is arranged; but as soon as the battalion shall be confirmed in the principles of the lesson, the fires will be executed after the advance in line, and after the various formations into line of battle, and into square. Particular attention

SCHOOL OF THE BATTALION.

will be given to the fire by file, which is that principally used in war.

Every lesson of this school will be executed with the utmost precision; but the second, which comprehends the march in column, and the march in line of battle, being of the most importance, will be the oftenest repeated, especially in the beginning.

Great attention ought, also, to be given to the fourth lesson, which comprehends the march in column by division, and the dispositions against cavalry.

The successive formations will sometimes be executed by inversion.

In the beginning, the march in column, the march in line of battle, and the march by the flank, will be executed only in quick time, and will be continued until the battalion shall have become well established in the cadence of this step.

The non-cadenced step will be employed in this school only in the repetition of the movements incident to a column in route, or when great celerity may be required.

When it may be desired to give the men relief, arms may be supported, if at a halt, or marching by the flank.

In marching by the front, arms may be shifted to the right shoulder; but not in the march in line of battle until the battalions shall be well instructed.

After arms have been carried for some time on the right shoulder, they may be shifted, in like manner, to the left shoulder.

When a battalion is manœuvring, its movements will be covered by skirmishers.

All the companies will be exercised, successively, in this service.

When a battalion, instructed in this drill, shall be required to manœuvre in the evolutions of the line, its movements will be regulated by the instructions contained in the third volume of the Tactics for heavy Infantry, approved by the War Department, April 10th, 1835.

TABLE OF CONTENTS

Vol. II.

TITLE FOURTH.

SCHOOL OF THE BATTALION.

	PAGE
Formation of the battalion (No. 1)	5
Composition and march of the color-escort (No. 4)	5
Honors paid to the color (No. 11)	7
General rules and division of the school of the battalion (No. 14)	7

PART FIRST.

ARTICLE I.—To open and close ranks (No. 22)	9
ARTICLE II.—Manual of arms (No. 30)	11
ARTICLE III.—Loading at will, and the firings (No. 31)	11

PART SECOND.

Page

ARTICLE I.—To break by company to the right (No. 69). Break by company to the left (No. 74). Break by division (No. 75). To break by company, marching (No. 84).................................. 18

ARTICLE II.—Break to the rear by the right or left of companies (No. 87). Break to the rear by the right or left of companies, marching (No. 94). Advance or retire by the right or left of companies (No. 105). Advance or retire by the right or left of companies, marching (No. 110). Advancing or retiring, by the right or left of companies, to form line to the front (No. 113).................................. 23

ARTICLE III.—Ploy the battalion into close column on the first division (No. 119). Ploy the battalion into close column on the fourth division (No. 141). Ploy the battalion into close column on any interior division (No. 143). Battalion being in march, to ploy it into column on the first division (No. 149).. 29

PART THIRD.

ARTICLE I.—March in column at full distance (No. 164). Column being in march, to execute the about (No. 170). Column arriving in front of the

PAGE

line of battle, to prolong it on this line (No. 175). Column arriving behind the line of battle, to prolong it on this line (No. 184). Column arriving on the right or the left of the line of battle, to prolong it on this line (No. 188). Manner of prolonging a line by markers (No. 189)........................ 37

ARTICLE II.—Column in route (No. 198)................ 48

ARTICLE III.—Change of direction in column at full distance (No. 231).. 55

ARTICLE IV.—Halt the column (No. 239)................ 57

ARTICLE V.—Close the column to half distance, or in mass (No. 252). Close the column on the eighth company (No. 267). Execute this movement, marching (No. 273).. 60

ARTICLE VI.—March in column at half distance, or closed in mass (No. 281).. 65

ARTICLE VII.—Change direction in column at half distance (No. 287)... 66

ARTICLE VIII.—Change direction of a column closed in mass, marching (No. 288). Change direction of a column, closed in mass, from a halt (No. 306)... 67

ARTICLE IX.—Take distances by the head of the column (No. 323). Take distances by the rear of the column (No. 333). Take distances on the head of the column (No. 341)... 73

ARTICLE X.—Countermarch of a column at full or half distance (No. 351). Countermarch of a column closed in mass (No. 352).. 79

	PAGE
ARTICLE XI.—Being in column by company, closed in mass, to form divisions (No. 364). To form divisions, marching (No. 376)....................................	81

PART FOURTH.

ARTICLE I.—Manner of determining the line of battle (No. 389)..	87
ARTICLE II.—To form a column, at full distance, to the left into line of battle (No. 390). To form a column to the right into line of battle (No. 399). A column being in march, to form it into line of battle (No. 402). To form a column into line of battle, and to move it forward (No. 403). By inversion to the right or left into line of battle (No. 407). Column at full distance, to form it on the right or left into line of battle (No. 414). Column at full distance, forward into line of battle (No. 440). Forward into line of battle, marching (No. 452). Column at full distance, faced to the rear into line of battle (No. 466). Execute this movement, marching (No. 479)....................................	87
ARTICLE III.—Formation in line of battle by two movements (No. 485)..	110

ARTICLE IV.—Different modes of forming column at half distance, to the left or right, into line of battle (No. 501). By the rear of column, left or right, into line, wheel (No. 503). Column at half dis-

tance, on the right or left, into line (No. 507). Column, at half distance, forward into line (No. 508). Column, at half distance, faced to the rear into line (No. 509)... 113
ARTICLE V.—Deployment of columns closed in mass (No. 510). Deployment on the first division (No. 514). To deploy, whilst marching, on the first division (No. 532). To deploy without halting the column, and to continue marching (No. 536). To deploy on the fourth division (No. 541). To deploy, whilst marching, on the fourth division (No. 556). To deploy on an interior division (No. 563). To deploy, whilst marching, on an interior division (No. 567).. 116

PART FIFTH.

ARTICLE I.—To advance in line of battle (No. 587).. 132
ARTICLE II.—Oblique march in line of battle (No. 623)... 141
ARTICLE III.—To halt the battalion, marching in line of battle, and to align it (No. 635)............... 143
ARTICLE IV.—Change of direction in marching in line of battle (No. 652)...................................... 146
ARTICLE V.—To march in retreat in line of battle (No. 664).. 149
ARTICLE VI.—To halt the battalion, marching in retreat, and to face it to the front (No. 676)........ 151

VOL. II.—20

	PAGE
ARTICLE VII.—Change of direction, in marching in retreat (No. 681)	152
ARTICLE VIII.—Passage of obstacles, advancing and retreating (No. 682)	153
ARTICLE IX.—To pass a defile, in retreat, by the right or left flank (No. 710)	159
ARTICLE X.—To march by the flank (No. 722)	162
ARTICLE XI.—To form the battalion on the right or left, by file, into line of battle (No. 735)	164
ARTICLE XII.—Change of front perpendicularly forward (No. 743). Change front forward on the first company, marching (No. 754). Change of front perpendicularly to the rear (No. 761)	165
ARTICLE XIII.—To ploy the battalion into column, doubled on the centre (No. 776). To form double column, marching (No. 787). Deployment of the double column, faced to the front (No. 796). Deployment of the double column, marching (No. 800). To form the double column into line of battle, faced to the right or left (No. 803). To form the double column into line of battle, faced to the right or left, marching (No. 807)	172
ARTICLE XIV.—Dispositions against cavalry (No. 817). A column being in march at full distance, to form square (No. 837). If the column be closed in mass, to make dispositions to form square (No. 847). The battalion being in square, to move it in advance by one of its fronts (No. 854). To halt	

TABLE OF CONTENTS. 231

the square (No. 860). The battalion being in square, to form column to march to the front, a distance greater than thirty paces (No. 863). To march the square in retreat a greater distance than thirty paces (No. 872). The battalion being in square, to march it in advance, or in retreat, a distance less than thirty paces (No. 876). The column marching to the front, to march it in retreat (No. 879). The column marching in retreat, to march it to the front (No. 881). To reduce the square (No. 883). To form square from line of battle (No. 885). Perpendicular square (No. 888). Perpendicular square, marching (No. 890). To form square by double column (No. 892). To form square by double column, marching (No. 894). Observations relative to the formation of squares in two ranks (No. 896). The column being formed of four divisions, to place the inner platoons of the third division in reserve (No. 898). Squares in four ranks (No. 910). The square formed in four ranks being reduced, and at a halt, to form the battalion into two ranks (No. 916). The column being in march with divisions formed in four ranks, to re-form it into two ranks (No. 920). To form square in four ranks on one of the flank divisions (No. 923). Form square in four ranks on the first division, marching (No. 928). Form perpendicular square in four ranks, by double column (No. 931).

	PAGE
Form perpendicular square in four ranks, by double column, marching (No. 935). Oblique square (No. 938). Oblique square, being in column (No. 945). Column against cavalry (No. 965). The battalion being no longer threatened by cavalry, to form column (No. 970)	182
ARTICLE XV.—The rally (No. 974)	213
ARTICLE XVI.—Rules for manœuvring by the rear rank (No. 979)	214

THE END.

Printed in Dunstable, United Kingdom